Happy Families

Also available from Network Continuum

Help Your Young Child to Succeed – Ros Bayley, Lynn Broadbent and Debbie Pullinger
Help Your Child to Succeed – Bill Lucas and Alistair Smith
Help Your Boys Succeed – Gary Wilson
Help Your Talented Child to Succeed – Barry Teare
Flying Start with Literacy – Ros Bayley and Lynn Broadbent
Success in the Creative Classroom – Steve Bowkett, Tim Harding, Trisha Lee and Roy Leighton

Available from Continuum

Help Your Child with Literacy 3–7 – Caroline Coxon
Help Your Child with Numeracy 3–7 – Rosemary Russell

Happy Families

Insights into the art of parenting

Steve Bowkett, Tim Harding,
Trisha Lee and Roy Leighton

network
continuum

Continuum International Publishing Group
Network Continuum
The Tower Building
11 York Road
London
SE1 7NX

80 Maiden Lane, Suite 704
New York
NY 10038

Cardiff Libraries
www.cardiff.gov.uk/libraries

Llyfrgelloedd Caerdydd
www.caerdydd.gov.uk/llyfrgelloedd

www.networkcontinuum.co.uk
www.continuumbooks.com

British Library Cataloguing-in-Publication Data
A catalogue record for this book is available from the British Library

ISBN: 9781855394476 (paperback)

Library of Congress Cataloguing-in-Publication Data

Library of Congress Cataloging-in-Publication Data

Happy families : insights into the art of parenting / Steve Bowkett
...[et al.].
     p. cm.
  ISBN 978-1-85539-447-6
 1. Parenting. 2. Parent and child. I. Bowkett, Stephen. II. Title.

  HQ755.8.H363 2008
  649'.1--dc22

2008019070

The Every Family Matters Programme was devised and created by MakeBelieve Arts. The actors appearing in the photographs are Nicole Charles, Jules Craig and Charlie Folorunsho.

Typeset by Fakenham Photosetting Limited, Fakenham, Norfolk
Printed and bound in Great Britain by MPG Books, Cornwall
Illustrations by Margaret Chamberlain

Contents

Dedications

Steve Bowkett

Thanks and appreciation to Roy, Trish and Tim for sparking ideas; to Jim for creating the Blue Duvetiers; and to my close friend Ben Leech for his hard work, loyalty and unfaltering faith in the power of stories.

Tim Harding

My chapter would, of course, have been impossible to write without experience of family music making. I am indebted to my family – Amanda, Emily, Charlotte and Eleanor (aka 'the neumes') not only for years of musical enjoyment and experiences, but also for their great help in the writing of this chapter, which has been a collaborative process.

Trisha Lee

To my son Callum, for reminding me to ask questions and to seek answers.

To my husband Bill, for his unrelenting support while I search.

Roy Leighton

To Angie, Lily, Ellie and Phoebe – my amazing wife and children who have helped me grow practically, intellectually, emotionally and spiritually. Thanks, ladies!

About the Authors

Trisha Lee is artistic director and founder of MakeBelieve Arts, a theatre and education company with a primary focus on storytelling and drama in the classroom. She has been delivering innovative approaches to the curriculum for the past 15 years, running teacher training sessions and programmes that encourage child-centred learning through drama.

Steve Bowkett is a full-time writer, trainer and creative writing tutor. He has 18 years' experience as an English teacher and has published 40 books including fiction for children and adults, and educational non-fiction.

Tim Harding taught in primary schools for 23 years, 15 of these as a headteacher, and is now a freelance educational writer and song-writer. He has frequently used music both as a dynamic starting point and as a medium for learning across the curriculum, and has written and produced a wide variety of music for primary school children.

Roy Leighton links the worlds of creativity, commerce and learning. Roy's work ranges from lecturing on complexity, confidence and organizational evolution to running sustainable development programmes for schools and businesses both in the UK and abroad.

'On Children'
from The Prophet by Kahlil Gibran

Your children are not your children.

They are the sons and daughters of Life's longing for itself.

They come through you but not from you,

And though they are with you yet they belong not to you.

You may give them your love but not your thoughts,

For they have their own thoughts.

You may house their bodies but not their souls,

For their souls dwell in the house of tomorrow, which you cannot visit, not even in your dreams.

You may strive to be like them, but seek not to make them like you.

For life goes not backward nor tarries with yesterday.

You are the bows from which your children as living arrows are sent forth.

Foreword by Sue Palmer

There's no right way to bring up children – just lots of parents doing their best to make a 'good enough' job of it. And since all children and all parents are different, each family's version of 'good enough' is necessarily different from all the others. So it's impossible to provide some sort of recipe for child-rearing that will work for everyone, and parenting manuals are eventually doomed to failure.

But in a fast-moving, market-driven, screen-based culture, there are problems to face and questions to answer that no previous generation of parents has ever had to deal with. Recent research from UNICEF, the Good Childhood Enquiry, the National Consumer Council and many other organizations makes it clear that parents can't just sit back and hand their children over to the media and marketers. There's plenty of evidence that constant exposure to a vacuous celebrity culture and the message that being 'cool' depends on endless mindless consumption isn't good for children's mental health.

So while there's no point in seeking a recipe, there are plenty of reasons for listening to good advice and ideas from people who've already negotiated the difficult path of twenty-first century child-rearing. Most parents today have little experience of children until they take their firstborn home from the hospital, and very few have access to the traditional support system of extended family and close-knit community – the people who, in the past, handed on ancient wisdom about how best to bring up a child.

The authors of this book are parents themselves – so they know all the problems and pitfalls – but they have the added benefit that each has worked with children for many years. So they also know about child development and the secrets of encouraging youngsters' creativity, self-discipline and love of learning. Between them they offer parents reassurance, encouragement, philosophical perspective and a wealth of practical advice for raising happy, balanced children.

Sue Palmer
Educational consultant and author of *Toxic Childhood*

Introduction

Journeys

We started the Blue Duvet group in 2004, at which time it was simply a group of eccentric creative educationalists who came together to share their disparate skills and look for common ground. It proved to be a great delight to me as the original convenor of the group to witness the exciting intellectual sparring that ensued. As time moved on, the group cohered and found much of the sought-for common purpose, initially in conversation and progressively in their writing. This resulted in the publication of their first book *Success in the Creative Classroom*, which is a delightful compendium of creative ideas for teachers to employ to enliven and broaden their teaching repertoire. The key thing that unites this group is a common belief that empowered learners can achieve amazing things if only teachers, parents and carers have the confidence to provide a rich and supportive environment for the learners to creatively explore their own talents.

It is fascinating to note that while the group itself has been on a creative journey, this is the very metaphor each of the authors alludes to in their individual chapters of this inspiring book. Trish takes us through the power of drama, Steve through the power of story and Tim through the power of music to assist us in aiding our children's journey towards adulthood. Roy brings all of this together in the final chapter, referencing his own personal journey with teachers, students, business people and other professionals. There is no manual for parenthood, but there are a lot of good ideas and pointers and this book contains many sources of such inspiration.

This present book in fact follows the same vein as the book for teachers mentioned above but takes a focus on that most challenging of activities – parenting young children and adolescents. I was reminded of the ethos of the group a couple of years ago when, out of the blue, I received a thank-you card from a taxi driver called Steve, who wrote:

'Remember me, I'm Steve the taxi driver who conveyed you from Lichfield to Stafford in March last year. During the journey I told you about Harvey, my 5-day-old grandson and my wish to be the greatest grandad the planet will ever see.

You talked about "Learning" – a personal journey, and everything you told me is proving to be spot on. My journey is 12 months old now, and there's hardly a day goes by when I don't see the Little Man and I can tell you he's a "Live Wire" as you would expect.

Jim, I want to say thank you to you for being you. It's with your words of wisdom and Harvey's zest for life I'm on one hell of a journey, "learning" as I go.'

This note was accompanied by a delightful photo of Harvey, demonstrating that very zest for life. I'm now a grandad myself and in turn take inspiration from Steve's words to make sure that I make as much of a contribution to Joseph's life as I can, continuing on my own learning journey, like Steve.

This book is a much greater store of wisdom about how we can help our children, and grandchildren, grow up and develop than my words to Steve could ever have been. This is actually the book that I wish I had been able to give him at the time; but I will certainly make sure that he gets one of the first copies of it in the certain hope that it will help him further on his learning journey.

Bon Voyage, Steve and Harvey!
Jim Houghton

Managing Director of Network Educational Press (NEP) 1993–2006

Introducing Trisha Lee – *by Jim Houghton*

Trish was always the one who focused the discussion back into what actually happens in the classroom and what works with real children. This assertion was grounded in working creatively with children on an almost daily basis with an ever-growing group of enthusiastic colleagues in an exciting social enterprise called MakeBelieve Arts, based in Lewisham, London.

It was Roy who actually introduced me to Forum Theatre and the power that it has for allowing people to engage with situations and issues from a different perspective. However, it is Trish who clearly uses it very frequently in her work with MakeBelieve Arts with many different groups, but particularly including parents and their children. The anecdotes that she describes in this first chapter are ones that will resonate with many parents, making us realize fundamentally that we are not alone in all the difficult issues we have to resolve. She also shares many of her own experiences of parenting, with its trials and excitements, and promotes the perhaps all too obvious concept that we can't be good at everything and sometimes we need friends and relatives to help us out.

Of course the real way to benefit from this kind of thinking would be to join existing Forum Theatre groups or even set up your own with skilled practitioners so that you make your own discoveries. However, there is a great deal to learn from these collected reflections that should spark off a variety of insights into how we can better help the children we care for. Indeed, my grandson Joseph's mum finds a lot of sustenance from her Mum's group where these kinds of reflections are shared and discussed. It's the honesty and frankness of such discussions that makes them so powerful.

To find out more about the work of MakeBelieve Arts please visit
www.makebelievearts.co.uk or email; info@makebelievearts.co.uk
Trisha Lee is a social enterprise ambassador.

chapter one

An elephant on my shoulder: The burden of parenthood

I thought it was just me?

Do you really feel like that?

Does your child do that too?

Is that what's happening in your head?

I thought it was just me?

Normally when we start a new job we are given training, support, wages, even a probationary period which is our chance to find out about the work involved, possibly realize that we've made a huge mistake and leave, no hard feelings.

But when we become a parent, no-one shows us what to do. There is no manual or job description that arrives with the little bundle. There's not even an off switch for those moments when we just need a break. We're even expected to take them away on holiday with us!

For women, hormone changes in our bodies give us some indication of the work that is in store for us, men don't even have that. But for both parents, male or female, having a child can be a huge shock. From the moment they are born they have their own likes, dislikes, wants and needs that don't always fit in with the way we hoped they'd do things.

Also as soon as we embark on having a baby we realise that we are entering a world that is brimming with the dreaded 'Opinions of Others'. Everyone is a self-elected expert.

From speculation as to what sex our child is going to be by the way the mother is carrying her pregnancy, down to the safety of scans, tests and the best location for the birth of the child. And all of this is nothing compared with the 'Opinions of Others' we receive (whether we ask for them or not) as soon as our child is born and we start taking it out.

'Oh his hands look cold; he really ought to be wearing gloves', says the stranger who has felt confident enough to grab my child's hands, feel them and then advise me on parenting. The fact that my child screams the minute you try to put gloves on him to the minute you take them off is neither here nor  there. This is the opinion of her mother and her mother before and she feels duty bound to pass it on.

And then, just as we think we've got used to it, for those of us who have second children, along comes another one who has a totally different personality and way of doing things and the whole learning process starts all over again.

Even if we only have one child, each different stage of growing up is a whole new journey of discovery. The fact is, that one day it's fine for us to hug and kiss our child in public and then before we know it we're told that it is 'uncool; and can you just drop me around the corner so none of my mates can see?'

A parent of a Year 6 girl spoke about her experience of this. 'The other day I was out with my daughter having a lovely time, and then in the distance she saw some of her mates, and to my sadness she let go of my hand. I felt really rejected.'

Mothers, often more than fathers, are lucky enough to make contact with other new parents when their babies are first born and these early friendships can be vital links for us in discovering how we parent. But as our children get older these important points of reference begin to fade. The mothers who sat drinking cups of coffee together during those first few months of their babies' lives, discussing the smallest rash and exchanging tips on colic, or where to buy the cheapest or the most environmentally friendly nappies, the joys of nappy-free time, have often returned to their lives, their jobs, their old friends. And we are suddenly left with no manual and a child who expects us to know everything.

A place to talk

Having begun to realize the importance of creating a place for parents to talk openly about the issues surrounding parenting, I was delighted when Lewisham Extended Services approached me, through MakeBelieve Arts, to develop a programme exploring some of the issues that we as parents face when our children are about to start school, both primary and secondary, for the very first time.

I decided I wanted to create two pieces of forum theatre that would contain some of the issues that all of us have found ourselves facing during these times of transition in our children's lives.

In Forum Theatre the audience watches a selection of scenes that in some way relate to their experiences and that also present a range of problems for one or more of the characters.

The audience, or spect-actor as they are called by Augusto Boal who created this technique, then have the chance to get up on stage and change the action. Their role is to try to find solutions to the problems presented in the scenes, not by creating magical answers, but by finding realistic ways of challenging the views of the people involved.

During the tour we spoke to hundreds of parents about their view on parenting.

We were surprised about how many things the parents in our audiences had in common:

- None of them believed whole heartedly that they were doing a brilliant job of parenting.

- All of them had some degree of guilt about their parenting style and methods.

- A lot of them admitted to a deep-down anxiety that their approach to parenting was fundamentally flawed.

- Everyone we spoke to agreed that parenting is probably one of the hardest jobs we will ever get to do.

- After the show everyone went away with a feeling of relief, having said to themselves for the last few years 'I thought it was just me'.

As one parent said to us after seeing the performance at a local secondary school, 'If we were all in this room and we didn't have this it would be hard to communicate with each other. But this drama helps to bring people out of themselves and to talk to each other. We all need that, as parents, we so need that.' In the final chapter Roy talks in more detail about how as adults we need to continue to evolve, to question, to learn, unlearn and relearn. The audiences we worked with all felt that they entered an arena where they could evolve, where they engaged with examining how things were in their lives and had the opportunity to discuss and physically enact possible solutions that might create a more harmonious environment, unlearning and relearning.

Every Family Matters

MakeBelieve Arts developed two Every Family Matters shows, one for parents of 5 year olds and one for parents of 11 year olds. Each show was performed by a team of three actors, two females and one male. They portrayed a range of characters, including the two key families; a single parent mother with two children and a mother and father who live together with their one child.

The stories centred on the parents at key points throughout their day; breakfast on a school morning, homework and bedtime. Within the scenes we incorporated many issues including the role of fathers, education, anxiety and guilt.

One of the interesting discoveries we made while we were creating both shows was the realization of how many issues continue to be problematic for us as parents even as our children get older. Of course there are huge differences, particularly in the way we behave with our children at different stages in their development and our changing expectations of them, but certain times of the day continue to act as triggers between parents and children regardless of age.

The Every Family Matters shows toured for a period of five weeks around primary and secondary schools where new parents of Reception, Year 1 and Year 7 were invited to attend.

Our audiences were made up of parents from all different backgrounds and walks of life. Many of them had seen very little theatre and quite a few confessed to us at the end of the session that they had only intended to pop in for a few minutes to show willing and then they had planned to sneak off unnoticed. Everyone who said this to us added that they had become so engrossed in the performance and the issues it brought up that they had surprised themselves and stayed for the whole session.

What happened in these audiences was incredible. Better than any of us could have expected ...

Once parents started to open up about their experiences, once one person was brave enough to say how they felt, what their child was like, how they dealt with or failed to deal with the problem, then the debating, the getting up on stage and having a go at changing the action, the level of discussion, of coming together to find a solution was phenomenal.

This kind of theatre catches like wildfire – the whole audience as one voice wants to tell their story.

When we create an environment where parents can be honest about what they feel these are some of the things that they say ...

Often people pretend that everything is fine when really it's not. We should be able to speak truthfully about how hard it is to be a parent.

Looking at the play it was a reflection of my life, I recognized everything in it and it was useful to know this happens to everyone. But also to get the chance to see it from a distance.

It was just like my home and the interaction with my child. Have you been watching me?

It's easy to be calm and rational when you have all these eyes on you. But it's not like that with your own child. They are you, they come from you and they are your babies. So your feelings are stronger, more difficult to control.

When we listen to other people's stories we realize that we are not alone. And yet how often do we give ourselves the luxury of talking honestly about being a parent and how it really makes us feel? How often do we have the chance to say what we find difficult without worrying that we are going to look bad?

Mirror, mirror on the wall, is my parenting any good at all?

Guilt

I went to see a friend of mine who was pregnant recently and when she opened the door I could tell that she had been crying. When I asked her what was wrong she burst into tears again.

'I'm such a bad mother', she shouted through her tears. 'How am I supposed to look after this baby properly when it arrives, when I can't even look after the scan photos? What am I going to tell my child, when all the other mums and dads are showing them their scan pictures. And my poor kid doesn't have any?'

It turned out that she had absent-mindedly left them on the tube and had been phoning lost property ever since, but they never showed up. Welcome to the world of parental guilt. I tried to tell my friend that if that was the worst thing she ever did, then her child would have a pretty bliss-filled life, but I could recognize that kind words weren't enough; that she had just had her first bitter taste of a world where you never quite feel that you are good enough.

Being a parent is so much about guilt. You constantly feel guilty. Sometimes I cry myself to sleep worrying about how I'm coping as a mother. Some days I just don't think I do it very well.

Sometimes I realize that I am being selfish because I am putting my needs before the needs of my children. But sometimes I just want my own space and time, and I find my kids so demanding. But then I feel guilty for even thinking that.

(Quotes from parents involved in the Every Family Matters forum theatre tour)

When I was in my early 20s I remember reading a book entitled *My Mother, My Self* by Nancy Friday. Her words on the first pages of that book had an enormous effect on me and stayed with me into my own parenting experiences. Talking about her relationship with her mother she begins the chapter:

> 'Sometimes I try to imagine a little scene that could have helped us both ... my mother calls me into the bedroom ... putting her hands ... on my shoulders she looks me right through my steel rimmed spectacles. "Nancy, you know I'm not really good at this mothering business," she says. "You're a lovely child; the fault is not with you. But motherhood doesn't come easily to me. So when I don't seem like other people's mothers try to understand that it isn't because I don't love you. But I'm confused myself ... We'll try to find other people, other women for you to talk to and fill in the gaps. With their help, with what I can give you, we'll see that you get the whole mother package. It's just that you can't expect to get it all from me ..."'

How many of us as parents feel confused, or feel like we're not quite able to deliver the whole parenting package, that we don't always know what to do for the best. In any job we have experts, specialists, people who are good at one aspect of the work, who we call on for their skills and experience where our knowledge doesn't quite stretch. Why is it as parents we beat ourselves up for not being good at all the things our children demand from us?

I love the honesty of the phrase, 'not seeming like other people's mothers ...' When my son was younger I became friendly with a woman who had a son of the same age. She was one of these highly organized people and it reflected in her parenting. I used to joke that her son played with his toys in straight lines, and I would find myself sneaking over to her house at all sorts of inappropriate times of day, unannounced, with some excuse or other, just to see if I could catch her place in a mess, or her not quite coping with the task of mothering. I never did manage it, and I laugh at myself now for my determination to find a crack in her armour, and my fascination with her orderly world which I was never quite able to reproduce.

How many of us have an image of parenting that we feel we should be attaining? Maybe it's based on a friend, our own parents, or a fictitious idea of what perfect parenting equates to. And how many of us, when children enter our lives get surprised at the extent of the chaos that comes with them?

How great it would be to turn around to our children, like Nancy Friday's fantasy of her mother and tell them that we know we won't always get it right, that being a parent doesn't always come easily and that during these times we will try to find other people who are better equipped to act as their guides or mentors. How great it would be to admit that we don't know it all, that we do make mistakes and that sometimes we get it wrong. Immediately I can feel the pressure begin to lift.

> If you feel guilty about how you parent then surely you should change your parenting style, it's more important that you're happy ... your kids are with you for the rest of your life, if you're not happy about something to do with parenting then that's a long time to be miserable.
>
> I'm a grandma now, and what it made me realize is that as a parent I was so het up. Children have their own time. Now I'm more relaxed; you are as you get older. And the more relaxed you are the easier it is. Children do things at the speed they do things, sometimes we just need to learn to wait.
>
> (Quotes from parents involved in the Every Family Matters forum theatre tour)

Children have their own time ...

But living our lives at the speed of a child is not always possible. Some days our own needs stop us being responsive to the needs of our children, and other days it's the external pressures that get in the way of our children's preferred timetable.

Morning routine

Single Mum:	I managed to get Tommy to school and Natalie to nursery on time every day for the first two weeks, but then my routine began to slip …
Mum:	Tommy, get downstairs and have your breakfast …
Natalie:	Mummy, Tommy's eaten my banana.
Mum:	Tommy, go and get your jumper, go and get your jumper now.
Tommy:	Mummy where's my jumper mummy?
Mum:	Natalie don't take your clothes off, were going to school in a minute.
Natalie:	Mummy I don't feel well.
Mum:	Tommy, Jumper!!! Get off of that play station … Okay Natalie, go upstairs and brush your teeth, good girl. Look at the time! Tommy, get your book bag. Where's my keys? Tommy, Book Bag!
Tommy:	Where is my book bag mummy?
Mum:	I don't know! Where are my keys? Right we've got to go now or we're going to be late!!!
Tommy:	Mummy can I bring my spider-man?
Mum:	I said, we've got to go, now.
Tommy:	Mummy I haven't got my dinner money, you forgot to give it to me …
Mum:	Tommy! Why didn't you remind me earlier, I haven't got any change, you'll have to tell them you'll bring it in tomorrow.
Tommy:	But mum, you said that yesterday.
Mum:	We're going to be late. Get yourself and your sister out of this house *now* …
Tommy:	But mum, I can't find my book bag …
Mum:	Right!!!!
Narrator:	The angry monster snarled and snarled at the little boy who ran and ran as fast as he could, back to the school building, where he sat in the corner and all he could think of all day long was the crossness of the face.
Teacher:	Tommy you're late, the register's already gone downstairs. You'll have to go down to the office and let them know you're here
Tommy:	Yes miss.
Teacher:	And don't forget to let them know you're having school dinners.
Tommy:	Yes miss.
Teacher:	Have you brought your dinner money in today?
Tommy:	No miss.
Teacher:	Tommy! Why ever not?

So many of the parents we spoke to empathized with the morning scene. At one primary school a father put up his hand and said that the problem was just one of routine and organization, something that our single parent mum was obviously lacking. We invited him on to the stage to take the place of our mum, working with our two actors in role as Tommy and Natasha. Every time he searched for Tommy's book bag, Natasha took her shoes and socks off, every time he put Natasha's shoes and socks on, Tommy hid his book bag. Within a few minutes the guy was at his wits' end. We stopped the scene for his own sanity and asked how he felt.

'It's a lot different with two children isn't it?' he remarked, 'I've only got one, and I'm not normally around for the school run. I can't believe how hard that was ...'

At another primary school a mother in the audience had needed to bring her toddler with her. 'That mum needs to talk to her children more, get them on her side, make them see why she wants them to get ready quickly, maybe then they will help her.'

When she got up on stage she brought her toddler with her and suddenly our family of two children became a family of three. Holding her daughter in her arms she expertly tied up the shoes of our actor Natasha before proceeding to put some structure into the scene in a way that surprised our actors for its kind but firm manner and had them eating out of her hand.

One of the issues the breakfast scenes made us all reflect on was the implications for our children when things do go wrong and we end up getting them to school late. Many parents commented on how they felt for Tommy when he arrived late having been shouted at that morning by the angry monster. But how hard it is to not show our cross faces when just as we're about to leave the house the unpredictable happens. The baby vomiting on the carpet just as you are about to open the door, turning around and finding your three year old totally naked when you only dressed her a few minutes ago, realizing you can't find your keys ...

Another issue for us parents when our children start school is that suddenly an outside agency is setting the timetable for them, which we have to fall in line with. No longer can we just work to our own timetable; children have to be at school on time every morning. There is no waking up and deciding we want to take a day off and go out for a treat, we have to wait for the school holidays for that. Suddenly something else is setting out our routine.

> You can't always keep to routine. When you're tired, had a bad day, when someone's cut you up on the road, you just want to relax when you get home, routine just disappears. It's always when I'm most tired that my mother-in-law gets involved and suddenly there are three people with different ideas stating how it should be. It's tough …
>
> (Quote from parent involved in the Every Family Matters forum theatre tour)

'It feels like I'm carrying an elephant on my shoulders …

We performed a similar version of the morning scene in the Every Family Matters show aimed at secondary school parents and just as it started a woman in the front row stood up and walked out. I was at the back of the audience and I watched her go, wondering if we had offended her. Seconds later she returned with her 11-year-old son. After the show she talked about walking out.

'The minute I saw what it was about I had to go and get my son from outside. That breakfast scene is identical to what happens in my house every morning and I wanted my son to see it from my point of view.'

When she got up to change the scene she called the actor in role as her son to the table and confessed that she hated shouting at him in the morning and could he just try and get ready for once without her needing to get cross. I found myself watching her son's reaction to this and you could see from the expression on his face that the message had hit home.

At another secondary parent show the school had invited some of their Year 7s to be part of the audience. On seeing the breakfast scene a mother spoke about how her son would try to be good in the morning and tell her to go and have a bath, but whenever she did, he would slow down so much that they would end up arguing. She had to get herself ready for work after he had left for school as it was the only way she could guarantee he would get to school on time.

Her son was one of the Year 7s in the audience. He asked if he could get up and try to change the scene. The actors laid it on thick for him, playing with the Playstation, moving very slowly. The boy tried getting cross with them, he tried doing everything for them, running around getting their books, making their breakfast, and then finally he offered them money, lots of money and suddenly the actors sped up and were out the door in seconds. When asked at the end of the scene how he had felt, he looked at his mum, then at the audience and said in a loud voice, 'It feels like I'm carrying an elephant on my shoulders.'

What a fantastic metaphor for those moments in parenting when we feel like we are struggling against the stream, trying to get our children to do things at a speed that they blatantly don't want to go at, or for those times when routine has disappeared and chaos has taken up residence in our homes.

Personally it's when I find myself involved in a frantic search through all those little hiding places that loose change congregate, trying to pull together enough money for school dinners on a Monday morning, that I know I've really blown any assemblage of good parenting for that day. And the thing that makes me most cross in the morning is my son's habit of handing me notes that need signing just as he is about to walk out the door – 'It's really important and it has to be in today.' Or the other great favourite is 'I need £2 for the science trip' or worse, 'I've got to have a packed lunch today …'

Maybe I'm my own worse enemy but I always find myself rushing around to make sure that all is in place to meet these needs, rather than just saying 'It serves you right for not telling me and you will just have to go without'. For me I find I have two choices, either make it right or face my arch enemy 'guilt' and I prefer a few minutes of quiet seething as I find the money, make the packed lunch, sign the form, to a day of worrying about the consequence for my son resulting from me following the techniques I'm sure any good behaviour therapist would recommend.

> The show made me think about how important it is for my daughter that I get her into school on time. I hadn't thought about the effect of my lateness on her. I've got to really start to prepare for the mornings. I put my keys down when I come in at night, and I'm lucky if I can find them again. No wonder my daughter loses things all the time.
>
> It was a great insight for me as a teacher who hasn't got children, into the things that parents are going through in the morning before they even get their child into school. I give parents such a hard time and yet some of them have three children all under 5. I don't think I could get that many children dressed and ready and out by 9am each morning.
>
> We all have bad mornings, what we need to have is people to talk to when we have those bad mornings, we all know what it's like, but we feel we have to pretend that bad mornings don't happen to us.

Education - Sending your child to school

If getting up in the morning and getting our children out of the door is a stress point, for some of us that is nothing compared with the anxiety that arises when our children start a new school for the first time.

First there's the choice, which school is best for the child? Then for some of us there are the difficulties of getting that choice. 'Do I live in the right street? Do I go to the right church? Is my child able to pass any entry exam requirements?' Even for those of us who don't feel as strongly about one particular school as other parents do, we all have opinions about the schools in our neighbourhood, and for most of us we probably have some knowledge of the so-called 'bad' schools, the schools we want to avoid for our child. But even these vary from parent to parent. I have seen parents screw up their noses about schools that I have worked in, where the catchment area is quite demanding but the dedication of the teachers and the creative approaches adopted to deal with the issues results in some of the best schooling around.

And once you've got the school for your child, there is all the worry, anxiety and guilt about whether it is the right one, and how your child will settle. Will they miss their friends from nursery or Year 6? Will they make new friends? Will the get lost? Will someone help them find their way around?

It's not my girl that seems to have the problem starting school. It's me. I can't believe how anxious I feel. I've had nightmares about it. I keep picturing her, sat on her own in the playground with no-one to play with. I don't want it to be like that for her . . .

(Quote from parent involved in the Every Family Matters forum theatre tour)

I remember when my son started primary school for the first time. I'd got everything ready the night before, and we'd done a practice run of the journey so that I knew how long it would take. I felt really excited for him.

As we entered the classroom I reached for his hand to reassure him, but he was off with barely a look back.

'Bye', I called out to him, but he was already playing with some Lego on one of the nearby tables and looking like he'd entered kiddie heaven. I remember looking behind me as I walked out of the classroom feeling neglected. Just hoping he'd look around, be a bit tearful maybe and show that he needed me. But a backward wave of his hand was all I got. Of course I was proud that he didn't burst into tears like some of the other children. But I would have liked to have felt important in his life as well.

In the primary Every Family Matters show the single parent, like me, watched her son happily skip off into the new world while she was left standing, feeling slightly flat and wanting a bit more reaction from him. We contrasted this with a scene from the other family.

Dad:	Don't forget 5 to 9 at the school gate, the Photo, it's historic. Take it just as she walks into the school. I wish I didn't have to go to work.
Mum:	I'll try my best.
Dad:	Please don't forget.
Dad (at work):	5 to 9, they should be at the school gate by now, I wish I was with them, I hope she remembers to take the Photo. I can see her now, my smiling happy daughter at the school gates.
Estelle:	Muuuuum, waaaaaaaaaaaaah, I don't want to go!
Mum:	It will be alright darling, it'll be alright.
Estelle:	I want to stay with you mummy!
Mum:	You are going to be fine.
Estelle:	Noooooooooooo mummy! I don't want to go with the lady!!! Mummmmmmmmmy don't make me …
Dad (at work):	Five past nine – no photo – right (calls his wife) Hello love, did you get the Photo? What do you mean No? What do you mean she's bawling her eyes out? What do you mean you didn't get to take the Photo? (hangs phone up) I knew I should have been there …
Narrator:	And her's weren't the only tears cried that day. For the tears of the child set of the mum who then set off the other mums who then set off their children, and before long the ground was awash with tears that swept the children away, over the hills, until they came to a strange building. As the door opened, out stepped a woman who beckoned to them
Teacher:	Welcome, come in, I have a coat peg here with your name on it.
Narrator:	But the door was closed to the mums and dads, to the anxious parents creeping back across the playground to watch through the gap in the window and see how their child was coping with their first day at school.

Many of the audience related to the parents watching through the windows to see how their child was doing. For all of us there can be a very real sense of a door shutting when our children start primary school.

> When my child started school, I used to watch through the window with the other parents and I saw my son was doing fine. Then he saw me through the window. I must have looked worried cos then he started to look worried and be anxious, and then he started crying. I don't look through the window no more.
>
> (Quote from parent involved in the Every Family Matters forum theatre tour)

Starting secondary school is no less anxious a time, and where primary school can feel like a door shutting, secondary school can feel like the door has been slammed in our faces, locked and then hidden from view. No longer can you get to speak to a teacher in the morning if your child is upset and no longer does your child confide in you as openly. Secondary school parenting can feel like groping in the dark.

I laughed out loud while reading John O'Farrell's satire 'May Contain Nuts' in which his central mother character is so neurotic about finding the right secondary school for her child that she decides to dress herself up as an 11 year old and sit the school entry exam.

For this mother 'the fear has many forms. When I was not worrying about something happening to my children, I worried that nothing would happen to my children. That they would end up as failures or embittered dropouts because we had neglected to give them the best possible start in life. That by the time he was a teenager Jamie would end up bunking off school and spend his days lurking on the London Underground with other feral street urchins, riding up and down escalators sticking chewing gum on the nipples of the girls in the bra adverts. And all because we'd mistimed the right moment to start clarinet lessons. So my children had to get the best education possible … The spectre of big school loomed out of the sky like those approaching asteroids, beginning as a tiny far-off dot but growing ever closer, rapidly blocking out light and warmth' (p. 65).

Farcical as this is, it is rooted in worrying truth and I found it hard not to relate to the mums' neurotic anxiety while at the same time swearing that I would never act like this as a parent.

When my son was about to start secondary school, I must have given him such a long list of things to watch out for and not to do, that he turned around to me one day and said, 'You think that the moment I walk into my new school I'm going to be offered drugs, given knives, get my head kicked in and then find myself a gun?' As he looked at me for an answer I couldn't deny it. Although I knew what he was saying was totally irrational, and actually I was really happy with the secondary school he was going to, I still felt afraid. I looked at him for a while, screwed up my face and nodded. It was true, my son starting secondary school made me highly anxious. I had to confront all of my worst fears.

For some of the project we worked in the afternoon with Year 7 pupils, showing them the performance and involving them in changing the action. We asked what they thought parents might feel once their children started secondary school. One girl piped up, 'Like they're in an empty space …'

Homework

I have always been struck by Winnie the Pooh and the way that A. A Milne records Kanga's approach to mothering in the book 'Tiggers Don't Climb Trees' from the collection entitled *The House at Pooh Corner*.

'Now it happened that Kanga had felt rather motherly that morning, and Wanting to Count Things – like Roo's vest and how many pieces of soap there were left …'

I really like the idea that some mornings we wake up and feel rather motherly. I know it's true for me. Some mornings when the sun is shining and everything is in order it's very easy to feel motherly and do 'Counting and Things'. For me it's when in my mind I fall into the role of the woman in the polka-dot dress, who lives in a cottage with a picket fence and bakes fresh bread every morning with my children happily weighing out ingredients besides me.

Feeling motherly happens on days when we feel okay about setting out paints and paper, to hell with the mess, when we can patiently look at maths homework we don't understand and go on the internet to find out the right way to do it in order to pass on our newly acquired skills, when we have the patience to listen to our child struggling with their reading.

As soon as I sit down to watch TV my son will come and ask me to read. It always happens. So I get the book and read to him. I work nights, my wife takes them to school in the morning and I pick them up. It's hard if it's just one parent, we share things, but sometimes I just want to say 'be quiet, let me watch the telly'

(Quote from parent involved in the Every Family Matters forum theatre tour)

Single mum:	Reading was a nightmare; I never seemed to have time to do it properly.
Natalie:	Mummy, Mummy, Mummy I'm hungry.
Single mum:	I know you're hungry love, and it's nearly dinner time, you'll just have to wait five minutes. Go and watch your DVD, go and watch Postman Pat ...
Tommy:	Mummy, mummy, mummy can I read to you? Please mummy.
Single mum:	Not now Tommy we're about to have dinner.
Tommy:	Oh please mummy.
Single mum:	No.
Tommy:	Oh please.
Single mum:	NO, we're about to have dinner.
Tommy:	All the other mums listen to their children reading.
Single mum:	Alright, we'll read just for five minutes. Are you okay Natalie?
Natalie:	Mummy?
Single mum:	What love?
Natalie:	Mummy can I have a digestive biscuit?
Single mum:	Not now love, we're about to have dinner, aren't we? We're going to have potatoes and sausages and beans, so you just wait, watch the telly, look at Postman Pat, and look at the little cat, they're funny aren't they? You like reading don't you Tommy? Okay ... off you go ... Well what's that first word there Tommy, just that little word? What's that little word?
Tommy:	T.
Single mum:	That's the first letter isn't it Tommy? T. What's that next letter then?
Tommy:	H.
Single mum:	H that's right, and that last one there?
Tommy:	E.
Single mum:	So what's the word Tommy, what's the word it makes?
Tommy:	T – H – E T – H – E
Single mum:	The – the
Tommy:	The
Single mum:	That's right, good boy. Now this next one's quite long: Cccch ch ch ch ...

Tommy:	Ccch ch ch ch ch …
Single mum:	The chil – the chil – the chil
Tommy:	Chil chil
Single mum:	Try and look at the word Tommy
Both:	Chil chil
Natalie:	Mummy? Mummy?
Single mum:	Yes Natalie?
Natalie:	Mummy I need something to eat, my tummy's hurting.
Single mum:	I know you need something to eat, we're going to have tea any minute now Natalie, so just you wait.
	The children!
Tommy:	Children.
Single mum:	Good, alright, what's this one?
Both together:	w, www, www, wwww
Single mum:	Were!
Tommy:	Were
Single mum:	The children were noisy, look at those noisy children, it's quite a long book now Tommy, so let's just do one more page alright.
	Look. This is easy because this is the same word, all of these words are the same except for the last one, so what's this little word? Hang on a minute …
Tommy:	Mummy don't go.
Single mum:	I'm coming back Tommy, I was just turning the dinner down.
	What's that word?
	It's 'the'.
	We've just done that word haven't we, it's just a little word. Look, it's there, it's just the same as the one on this page,
	THE

The, children, the children were noisy, look, the, children, were, messy, the, children, were, untidy, oh dear said Mrs May – that's another part of the story, we'll do this another time.

Natalie: Mummy I'm hungry ...
Single mum: I know!!!!!

The laughter of recognition when we ran this scene reassured us that at some time most of us as parents have felt uptight while listening to our children read. Watching our children struggle can be painful. We want to make it right, but we also know that sometimes they need to find the answers themselves. Add to that our own needs: the TV programme we really want to watch, the fact that we're tired after a long day and just want to switch off, anxieties we may have about money, or family, or work, and yet as parents we are asked to put all of these thoughts behind us and like Kanga, do counting and things.

Many parents got up and tried solutions to this scene. These ranged from bringing the child into the kitchen to read so that the mum could do both cooking and reading at the same time; which although very funny to watch often resulted in the mum having an even more frantic time than the one we'd created for her, to negotiating with the child about finding a regular slot for reading that suited everybody in the family.

The other scene we showed with the primary school parents was another mum using flash cards while her 5 year old displayed obvious signs of boredom. The mum tried really hard to engage her daughter and make the learning fun, but her daughter wasn't joining in. In the scene we gave the little girl a book that she had bought home from school. The book had no words in it, only pictures, but the mum in our story didn't approve of the book because she felt that her child should be reading.

Dad: It's what they are doing at school.
Mum: But how can she learn to read with a book with no words in it, it's ridiculous. What kind of school sends a book home that has no words?
Narrator: But the little crocodile didn't like it when the big crocodile did words with her, cos the big crocodile did snap and snap and snap until all the words disappeared off the page and flew away to the school building, where words hid secretly in pictures and sneaked out on readers when they were least expecting them.

It's hard when we don't understand why the school is making our children do things in a way that is different to how we would approach it or even how we were taught. Picture books are great ways of helping our children engage with books, discover secrets in the illustrations and help them with speaking and describing what is happening just from the images. They can be amazing starting points for invention, involving children in telling the story of the picture, creating their own reasons for why one character is sad, or another is cross. Pictures can be the beginning of a great adventure, but how many of us as parents want our child to be reading and don't really see the benefits of talking about what is happening in a book, rather than getting fixated on the words?

Reading in my house had times when it was painful, when I physically hurt with all the emotions I was feeling and trying to control as my child struggled with words that I knew we'd looked at a dozen times.

I remember clearly how even a page with only a few words could feel like a novel as we struggled through it, losing sense of the meaning of the story because of the lengths of the gaps between each of the words. I remember knowing that we ought to be reading two or three pages a night, but after what felt like hours of struggling through the first page I would find myself taking over and reading the next page myself. We ended up alternating, one page each, which was the only way we could get through the book.

Years later I spoke to a head teacher about this, and she said that if two people were reading *War and Peace* out loud, you wouldn't expect one of them to read it all. You would both take turns. I read one page and then you read the next. There may be fewer words on our children's pages, but the struggle to get through, to remember what is being said, equates it to a book of much larger proportions.

There is an exercise that was invented by Linda Pound, early years educationalist and author of *Supporting Mathematical Development in the Early Years* published by Open University Press, to demonstrate the difficulties children face when they are learning numbers for the first time. We used this before the show to warm the parents up.

Think of the words to the Grand Old Duke of York. We always invited the audience to say them out loud just to refresh their memories. And then we began the following test and asked people to shout out the answers as soon as they had worked them out.

In the nursery rhyme what word comes after the word 'them'? What word comes before 'ten'?

Say the rhyme starting with the word 'the' and missing out every other word.

Now try saying the rhyme backwards from the word 'men'.

If 'the' = 1, 'grand' = 2, 'old' = 3 etc., what is 'of' + 'had'? What is 'York' − 'grand'?

This might just seem like a bit of fun, but it is an excellent way of demonstrating what happens when children are learning. For us as adults if we were asked what number comes after 7 we would be able to answer the number 8 immediately. That's because number is firmly embedded in our brains, and we have instant recall on these types of questions. For children who haven't yet reached this state of instant recall we might as well be asking what word comes after 'them'? How many of us remember when we first learnt to count backwards having to work forward on our fingers first? And yet how easy it is for us now to count backwards from ten? Linda Pound's Grand Old Duke of York exercise is excellent for reminding us of the processes that our children are going though when faced with new activities that we now take for granted.

The thing that was special about the audience's response to these scenes was watching parents demonstrating the different ways they read with their child. Some parents recreated our scene, struggling with our actor in role as a child to try to get them to read properly. One woman having wanted to show our actor parent how to take more time over reading ended up flicking through the book exactly as our mother had to see how long it was. Other parents modelled fantastic storytelling techniques, one mum even going so far as to say 'forget about the words, tell me what's happening in the picture'. For more information on sharing stories with children, Steve's chapter later in this book is a goldmine of ideas.

The homework scenes for secondary school parents followed a similar vein, presenting an 11-year-old daughter struggling with her maths homework and eventually the mother and the father taking over, arguing about how to do it and pushing the daughter out of the way.

The problem is that often when our children are struggling with something and they come to us, the only way for us to help them solve it is by doing it ourselves so that we can then explain it to them. And this can sometimes result in us taking over.

I realized that I find it hard to watch anyone else searching for something on the internet because whenever they use a search engine the things that jump out when they scan read are different to the things I may find. This was really frustrating when I was helping my son recently with his history homework. I realized I could feel myself getting uptight as he read and opened up page after page on the computer. But as soon as I noticed it and joked openly about it, it became easier. I sat very firmly on my hands and watched him opening up different pages resigning myself to just helping by suggesting different search terms. He did his homework and I felt I'd supported him. Really he just needed me to show an interest; it was me that wanted to take over.

Bedtime

We all know the routine – my mate goes to bed at 12am, so why can't I? I guess if you know the mate's parents the sensible solution is to ask them. But bedtime in so many houses is a time of conflict. There always seems to be some sense of injustice felt amongst older children that their bedtime is different from everyone else's, and for younger children bedtime is the time when they suddenly remember all the wonderful and exciting things they want to do, or all the ailments and physical needs they must have fulfilled before they can possibly sleep.

When my son reached secondary school he went through a stage of not really talking to me about his day. I used to ask dozens and dozens of questions just to get some kind of picture of what was happening in his life. But then at bedtime he suddenly began talking again. For a while I fell into the trap of listening to him because it was such a relief to hear what was happening in his life and to enjoy chatting again. But also I was very aware of the clock and that this sudden openness was also just another bedtime stalling technique. Children are fantastically clever at sussing out their parents' weaknesses and playing on these to get their own way.

As a teacher I am often surprised when children tell me what TV programmes they have been watching. The bedtime routine is so important as otherwise children are tired in the morning. Tiredness has a huge impact on children's learning.

Sometimes I feel like crying when my daughter won't go to sleep. She says her eye hurts, her finger hurts, everything hurts, just so she can get out of bed.

(Quotes from parents and teachers involved in the Every Family Matters forum theatre tour)

Trying to establish a routine can be hard when two parents have different ideas about how this should work, or when one parent has a different time frame to the other due to their work commitments, as the following scene demonstrates. This was an issue that provoked much reaction from audiences wherever we performed.

(Mum, with great difficulty has just got 5-year-old Estelle off to sleep when her husband Anthony returns home from work.)

Dad: How's Estelle?
Mum: She's alright, a bit difficult this evening but she's alright.
Dad: I'll just pop up and see her for a couple of minutes.
Mum: Not now Anthony, please not now.
Dad: But I haven't seen her all day.
Mum: Anthony I've just put her down.
Dad: I've been at work all day darling, please, I just want to pop my head round the door, I won't wake her!
Mum: Please, leave it an hour, you know she wakes the minute you go near her. I'll make you a cup of tea …
(Mum goes into kitchen, dad delivers monologue)
Dad: I go to work all day, some weeks I do 40 to 50 hours, and then I come home and I want to see my daughter. I only want to see her for two minutes and yet she always tries to stop me. It's like no-one's listening to me and what I want. I'm her dad, I have as much right as everyone else to have a say in how she's brought up. And if I want to go and see my daughter when I come home from work of an evening then I can. I just feel so left out sometimes.
(Dad sneaks upstairs, kisses daughter who wakes immediately)
Estelle: (calls loudly) Daddy!
(Dad rushes downstairs and sits back down where he was before his wife gets back in the room)
Mum: Did you go upstairs?
Dad: No.
Estelle: (calls downstairs) Daddy, come back!
Dad: All right, Katherine, I went up there for two minutes, two minutes … is that so wrong?

Role of fathers

The scene above linked to the first day of school scene where the dad was not able to be present because of his work commitments. There was a lot of discussion between the men in the audiences about how hard it is sometimes for them to get time off work for things to do with their children that the women in a family may be able to get time off easier for.

For so many of the men in the primary school audience the bedtime scenario rang true. Many of them spoke about shift work, and not being there to put their children to bed. One husband and wife couple in the audience began a huge debate about the situation in their home, which resulted in them both coming up to try out solutions in the scene.

The husband worked shifts and often had to leave the house at 3am. He wanted to play the scene as if it was his life, with our actor child well and truly asleep during the small hours of the morning, with him sneaking in just to kiss her goodbye. He even took his shoes off as he neared the area of the stage that we had allocated as his daughter's bedroom and walked into the room on tiptoes. When he reached the door he looked at his sleeping child before entering and placing his hand on her shoulder to signify kissing her goodnight. Our mischievous actor immediately woke up with a look of joy on her face and uttered the fatal words, 'Daddy!' His wife in the audience told us that this is what often happens, 'He thinks he can sneak in and he won't get heard, but they wake up, and suddenly its 3am and you have children awake, and he has to go to work so I'm left to deal with it.' When the husband was asked what he'd hoped to achieve by his actions in the scene he laughed and said, 'I just hoped that I'd get away with it and that for once she wouldn't wake up.'

Next his wife came up to try out the action; she was incredibly strong with our actor dad. 'Yes you can go in and see your little girl', she answered, 'but I would prefer it if you didn't. I have struggled getting her to sleep, she always wakes the minute you go near her, and if you do go up, and she does wake up, then I am going out to a mate's, and I won't be home until late, so you will have to get her off to sleep again. Now do you want a cup of tea?' Our poor actor dad looked totally stunned and nodded placidly while the rest of the audience laughed.

This is a huge issue for me. I'm a musician. I'm always coming home late from gigs. My son always calls me on the phone to say goodnight. He tells me how many kisses I have to give him when I get home and he's asleep.

I do shift work. I understand the problems of the dad. I often don't see my kids at night and some days I don't see them at all. But I do Sundays, I cook, I look after the kid's; that's my day, Sundays.

I talk to my husband if he's going to be late, I get him to call my son so he can say goodnight.

Family time is not valued in this society ... the pressure of work, its hard when you're doing shift work, I never get to see my child except at weekends and then I'm too tired to be of much use

(Quotes from parents involved in the Every Family Matters forum theatre tour)

The reactions and involvement of parents to the issues we presented in both shows has been incredible. Nothing we were presenting was new or radical in any way, it was just a range of situations that we as parents had found ourselves in, in some way or another, since having children.

The way the audiences warmed up to the issues so quickly demonstrated that we were connecting with them. The vibrancy of the sessions was proof that here is a way of helping us to look at issues and worries we have about our children with other parents who we might not know and to realize that we are not alone.

We need to talk about how we feel about our children, we need to be able to tell our story, not because we are failing as parents, not because we feel that we are doing something wrong and need support, but because as soon as we begin to share our stories we realize that we have so much in common with each other.

I wonder if the best parenting comes with admitting we don't know. Maybe the best parenting happens when we take an anti-parenting stance. But what if we do admit to our children that we don't know what to do, or that we are feeling insecure or confused? Would that help us to develop as families because suddenly we are all responsible for the wellbeing of the household. I know I have found huge relief in the times I can admit to not having a clue. I know from my teaching when I do this with children of all ages we become a great team of problem solvers, trying to find a solution, trying out their ideas rather than imposing my own until often the best answers are a surprise to me.

Perhaps creative parenting is finding the story of the child who won't go to sleep or who won't do their homework? How does your child solve that problem? What are their solutions to the issues that worry you? Maybe their answers will throw up surprising solutions.

For me the other important thing I try to do is to not put down my child at the various stages of his learning. I remember being asked a few years ago 'Have you ever heard of Led Zep?' or more recently 'Do you know what drainpipe trousers are?' It's hard not to laugh, but I remember adults from my childhood continually going on about how none of our music was new, and how all of the things I was raving about they had already experienced, and it really annoyed me.

I was working in a nursery a few years ago and there was a 4 year old who every time she saw me told me the most amazing stories. One day I bumped into her mum who had come to pick her up, and in front of her daughter I said, 'Did you know your daughter is a fantastic storyteller?'

The mum looked at her daughter who was beaming with the compliment and turned back to me and said 'Yeah, she never keeps her big mouth shut ...'

Parenting has to be about allowing our children to blossom, to find out who they are and not about crushing their discoveries even if they are things we have already experienced. What was the inventiveness of our childhood? What are the stories that we have in our lives that our children might enjoy? We need to find time for more fun and games between parents and children, places where neither of us have to worry or be in control. As Tim demonstrates in his chapter later on in this book, 'The family that plays together stays together.'

An exercise in sharing

You may like to try this activity:

● Tell your child a story from your childhood.

● Then write down word for word a story told to you by your child.

● Next each of you draw a picture for each other's story.

There are no wrong or right answers in parenting. Each of us is different and each of our children respond differently to different stimuli. There are things that we may see other parents doing that would make us screw up our noses, but maybe the way they are doing things is right for them or right for their children. Philip Larkin believed that whatever we do we mess up our children. One of his poems states very clearly that your mum and dad 'fuck you up'. The poem goes on to assure us that though they may not mean to, they fill us up with all their faults.

I think that's a bit harsh, but I do understand the sentiment. As my child gets older I realize that the times when I most annoy him are the times when I am trying too hard to get it right. The times when my mum most annoys me are also the times when she is trying too hard to get it right.

Sometimes I feel that the best parenting I can do is to stand a little way off, watching from a distance as my child climbs up the various rungs of his life. Occasionally I won't be able to help myself and I'll call out 'be careful', but mostly I'll wait till he calls down and asks for help and I'll stand there ready, knowing if the worst comes to the worst I am just close enough that I can grab him if he falls.

Narrator: And as the adults peered in through the window of the school building, the glass began to frost and became like a mirror, and the only thing the people on the outside looking in could see, was a reflection of themselves, and the harder they looked the less they saw, until they learnt not to look so hard, and then on those days they would catch a glimpse of their children.

Introducing Steve Bowkett – *by Jim Houghton*

Steve is an old friend with a wicked twinkle in his eye. He is a storyteller (and indeed writer) par excellence. He talks in his chapter about the power of reading and sharing and making stories. My own grandson, Joseph, is now two and a half and you can almost see him building his vocabulary on a daily basis, imitating and rehearsing the things he hears in the conversations in the family and most recently at nursery. It is a real joy to join in the fantasy stories he makes up building up on his accumulating experience. The make-believe stories come in all shapes and sizes, like when Stripe, the soft toy zebra, is crying because he's cold and needs to borrow one of Joe's jumpers to keep warm or when he decides to bake an imaginary cake, putting in all the specified individual ingredients, like his granny does, but then shouts 'oops' with suitable gesture of hand across mouth, because he's forgotten to put it in the oven before eating it!

Steve explores these innate creative tendencies in all children in this chapter, giving plenty of documented research on the subject, but also giving lots of hints and support to parents and carers in helping to encourage and share in this natural activity.

Steve is indeed an expert in this area. I have seen him telling stories to groups of small children from some of the many books he has written for children. On one memorable occasion I saw the audience became completely enthralled in the story of how a group of boys, including one called Steve, were scrumping old man Jones' apples until one day he caught them red handed. The story had all the storyteller's devices, such as change of pace and certain details repeating to build familiarity and the incidental detail that the boy Steve scraped his leg in his escape. At the end of the story there were questions and insights into the story, and then the inevitable questions about whether the story was true and whether the author was in fact the boy Steve in the story. In the end, Steve had to roll up his trouser leg to demonstrate that indeed he did have a small scar on his leg; that's the power of storytelling.

chapter two

Three golden apples: The importance of sharing stories

'Three golden apples fell from heaven one day – one for the storyteller, one for the listener, and one for those who heard.' (Armenian Proverb)

'As a very little boy', Ben told me, 'I would come home from school on a Wednesday and Mum had cooked me pea soup, which I ate with bread. Then for dessert there would be a jam doughnut. After that I sat beside her and she would read to me from the comic book that we had delivered weekly. She got a bit impatient when I wanted her to read the same story again – sometimes for the third or fourth time – or when I spotted a bit she had skipped because she wanted to get on with her work. But she never lost her temper and an hour would go by in a flicker, and that quiet corner of the room was so cosy and filled with such love. I remember it very clearly nearly fifty years later ...'

The psychologist Lev Vygotsky said that 'Words play a central part not only in the development of thought but in the historical growth of consciousness as a whole. A word is a microcosm of human consciousness.' It was his firm belief that thought does not simply find its expression in speech, but its very form and reality. Without words, Vygotsky suggests, meaningful thought to any degree would be impossible.

Thought allows us to make sense of the world through linked networks of ideas. Such 'meaning making' is a result our own direct experience and is enriched by the experience of others that we hear second (or third or fourth) hand. Stories give structure to such experience. They offer meanings that we may accept wholeheartedly or we may modify and interpret them to fit in with our own belief systems. Or of course we can simply dismiss out of hand as brief entertainment. In this sense I am using the word story to mean the same as narrative. The roots of this word go back to the Latin *narratus* – 'to come to know'. By means of story we can travel to far and exotic realms (real or fantastical) and to familiar places that we may suddenly see anew. Stories are the vehicle we ride on through life – indeed, isn't it significant that we call our very existence in time a 'life story'? We can't help but think in terms of stories – what some philosophers call 'narratizing' – of beginnings, middles and endings, of scenes and chapters, of pace and mood and characters. Even the expression 'turning over a new leaf', where we make some important change for ourselves, refers to the flipping of a page and putting what has gone by behind us.

> 'Meaning making' is a phrase coined by the American media analyst Marshall McLuhan. He is quoted in Neil Postman and Charles Weingartner's influential book *Teaching as a Subversive Activity*[1]. Postman and Weingartner highlight the importance of creativity in learning and state that human beings are 'meaning-making creatures'.

Stories give us context and continuity. So how much more important are they for children, whose minds are growing so swiftly and for whom the world is such a mysterious, miraculous and sometimes frightening place? This chapter is about sharing stories with your children – the why and how of it – underpinned by the assertion that when you spend time doing that, your efforts will be rewarded with much fine fruit.

'Somewhere, something incredible is waiting to be known.' – Carl Sagan[2].

Why stories are important

The writer and educationalist Sue Palmer, in her powerful book *Toxic Childhood*[3], argues that there are three key abilities which help set children on the path to becoming well balanced, useful and creative members of society. They are –

1. The ability to maintain attention even if something is not immediately interesting.

2. The ability to defer gratification. That is, the wherewithal to suspend the impulse to be rewarded or satisfied now because they see beyond the immediate to greater purposes in the future.

3. The ability to balance one's own needs against the needs of others. In other words the ability to empathize and compromise. Roy has more to say about this in his chapter as he discusses the 'me-we' balance that must be maintained as we grow.

It's clear that all of these require the active use of imagination to see past the here-and-now of one's present circumstances. There are many reasons why so many children do not have these abilities or develop them to any great degree – indeed that is what Sue Palmer's book is all about. But there are also many ways in which they *can* be cultivated, not least through parents sharing stories with their children.

To be able to give attention, to defer gratification and to compromise mark out the civilized person. All demand tolerance, and it was Helen Keller who said that tolerance is the highest aim of education. When children are engrossed in a story they give attention effortlessly. True enough they don't need to try to be interested; a good story is absorbing anyway, but what better way of learning to attend to the uninteresting and mundane than by developing the attention habit pleasurably?

Helen Keller (1880–1968), blind and deaf American educator. She also famously said 'Life is either a daring adventure or it is nothing.'

Deferred gratification is not an all-or-nothing situation. Sometimes it's true that by taking nothing now we are fully rewarded later. If I cut out sweets, snacks and beer now maybe I'll reach my target weight ready for my holiday in a few months' time. If I sit and work at my computer today I can treat myself to a cinema trip tomorrow (no popcorn or hotdog though) … More often however deferred gratification blends into ongoing moderation, which is itself a kind of compromise. It is an important attribute too, in a society whose consumerist engine constantly seeks to drive us towards an I-want-it-all-I-want-it-now mentality. In his chapter Roy discusses how immediate gratification is a powerful force in children's development but how we must all grow beyond it to become more fully integrated members of society.

> Deferred or delayed gratification is the ability to wait to obtain something that you want. Such self-control is widely believed to be a strength or a positive personality trait. A much publicized experiment in deferred gratification was carried out by Walter Mischel of Stanford University in the 1960s. A group of four year olds were each given a marshmallow and were promised another if their didn't eat the first one for 20 minutes. Some children could control their impulse to eat the marshmallow but others couldn't. Mischel and his team tracked the children through to adolescence and demonstrated that the ones who could defer their gratification were better adjusted and more dependable (according to parents and teachers) and scored on average 210 points higher on the Scholastic Aptitude Test.

When we as adults share stories with our children we are teaching them to hold back immediate wants and needs and to actively look forward to later pleasures. Putting a definite limit on story time is a gentle discipline and a meaningful compromise: the child realizes that you have given up some of your time and the opportunity to do other things to be with her. There will be more stories tomorrow, but that's enough for today. Such rule making is important; Roy highlights this in his chapter. Incidentally, the word compromise means 'to promise together': there is a mutual understanding that each of you, parent and child, is giving something precious to the other.

When a child learns not to demand more of your attention; when they recognize the value of a set time for sharing stories, they are putting your needs before their own. Moreover they come to realize that different people have different needs. Maybe you have work to do now, or want to spend time with another person, or perhaps just simply to chill out by yourself. Furthermore, the way that stories are built means that all children have to wait patiently for the narrative to unfold before gaining the 'reward' of a satisfying resolution. It is expected, part of the unspoken ritual of being a participant in story, carrying with it the hidden learning that without the journey the idea of a destination is meaningless.

These insights on the child's part build into an attribute, a trait of personality and a social skill that is *transferable* to many other contexts. A child who is tolerant around story time will tend to become tolerant more generally – and what a treasure that is in an all too often intolerant world.

In that 'little golden pocket of time' when stories are shared you are offering your children the three most valuable things any parent can give – time, attention and love. Sue Palmer (and doubtless many other researchers in the field) maintains that these are the fundamental keys to successful parenting.

> 'But in vain we build a world unless the builder also grows.' Ancient Wisdom

Some years ago a librarian friend of mine wanted me to meet a boy who had gained a very bad reputation at his school. I was fine with that until I saw the kid she was talking about. He was a huge, massive-boned, bristle-headed youth who could barely shoulder his way in through the doors. Other kids moved aside through fear. He clumped his way over to us.

'This is Ryan', my friend said. 'Last year he was excluded from school twice for bullying, never did his homework, and his teachers were at their wits' end with him. I hope you don't mind me saying this, Ryan, but I wanted Mr Bowkett to know about your past difficulties. He's much improved now,' she added, glancing at me, 'because one day you were sent down to the library, weren't you? And you found a book you liked and you stuck with it. Now you're reading regularly. We're all very proud of that. Mr Bowkett wanted to congratulate you.'

'Oh, I certainly do.' I held out my hand without thinking and Ryan engulfed it in his own mighty fist and we shook hands like friends. His heavy pugilist's face broke into a smile.

'Fact is,' he said, with a new-found wisdom, 'it just takes the right story at the right time.'

More benefits

Perhaps you are already very aware of the great value of story sharing with your children, above and beyond the basic points that I have made. If so, all to the good; but possibly I can say a few things that are new to you. If you are only now thinking of adding the sharing of stories to your parenting skills, then let me try to persuade you further, and to the best of my ability, of the great benefits that it will bring ...

Interactive talk

Stories provide a common ground where parent and child can talk together, where thoughts and opinions are valued, where different viewpoints are appreciated and ideas explored. I have deliberately spoken about story *sharing* rather than you as a parent simply reading or telling stories to your child. As Tim argues in his chapter, children's active participation is so much more valuable than any amount of passive listening, while the power of the Forum Theatre work that Trish describes is that children and their parents actually get up on stage and improvise others' viewpoints, highlight problems and difficulties and seek new strategies and solutions.

When you tell a story well children will be actively engaged of course – but ask questions and seek opinions also. When your child feels that *they* have something worthwhile to say, and when they know that you are keen to listen, the value of your shared time increases greatly.

In their book *The Unfinished Revolution*, the authors John Abbott and Terry Ryan quote a study[4] which suggests that the most reliable indicators of a child's success in later education include how much conversation that child has with its parents before ever starting school, and how much exposure to books the child gets in the early years of schooling. No doubt this second 'predictor of success' is even more powerful when children are exposed to books and stories at home in the early years too.

Both of these factors refer to the richness and diversity of the environment of words, and how much opportunity children have to 'do language'. Much research indicates that we are all born into the world with the potential to master and manipulate ideas through language: it is one of our 'natural intelligences' – one of the basic ways in which we handle information in order to survive and to flourish[5]. Like the other intelligences, linguistic intelligence is a use-it-or-lose it ability; or at the very least one that if we don't use fully and in ways that challenge us, we don't develop to a very high degree.

Interactive talk is just that, actively speaking together where each responds thoughtfully to what the other says. Thus it is a learning process where information is exchanged and where mutual understanding develops. It is truly educative, where education means (from the Latin) 'to draw out and rear up'. When as a parent I draw out from my child what they think and why think it and when I value their ideas, then their confidence and thinking abilities increase and they are reared up to be an independent, self-assured and creative individuals.

Rehearsing the world

Stories don't have to be realistic or deal with 'issues' to offer insights into people, relationships or situations. A number of writing tutors I've met give the advice that budding authors should 'write what they know'. For a long time I pondered then on the value of Science Fiction and Fantasy stories (both as a reader and writer of them) and of fairytales and nonsense tales – until I came to realize that at deep levels we all share common human experiences, which can be expressed metaphorically through these genres. Stories lead us over this basic ground of being human, and of course they often serve as pathways that show us how to do it more successfully ...

Five-year-old Samantha was playing by herself at her playgroup, pushing a buggy and talking to her dolly as she walked around the playground. One of the supervising adults, Julie, thought that she would join in and talk to Samantha about her game. As Julie approached she could hear the little girl chatting away about what shops they must go to and what needed to be bought, and then all the things that had to be done at home afterwards … 'Hello you two', Julie said cheerfully. Then, leaning over the doll she added, 'Oh, but you're a pretty one aren't you? And what is *your* name?' At which point Samantha gave her a withering look and announced disdainfully, 'Julie, it's just a bit of plastic!'

What we know of the world and of ourselves comes in no small part from the stories we experience, including the ones we tell ourselves. As Trish observes in her chapter, in parenting as in so many other aspects of life there is no manual or job description that comes with the task. However, through stories we meet and rehearse (if only in imagination at first) the roles, rules, rights and responsibilities we might engage with later. Bearing in mind what Vygotsky told us, we create our world through our perceptions, and our perceptions through the words we use to frame our very thoughts. When we talk about children being 'in a world of their own', perhaps sometimes we fail to realize how profoundly true that is.

'What we see depends mainly on what we look for.' Sir John Lubbock

Maps and models

It is widely claimed by psychologists, and is a common lay belief, that none of our experiences are ever truly forgotten and lost. Rather, everything that happens to us is woven into an astonishingly complex web of subconscious memory that forms what is often called our 'map of reality'. Like any map it guides us along our way, and like any map it is not the territory itself. What we have in our heads is a representation of the sense we have made out of this chaotic cascade of events that we call human existence.

Stories are like roadways through the forests of life. First and foremost they allow us to realize that we are not alone and we are not the first. Whatever happens to us, other people have been there before us, and their stories can give us strength and also possible ways of dealing with similar situations if we encounter them ourselves.

Stories also offer role models on which children can, at least in part, base their own attitudes and actions. Sometimes experiencing just one story or character can be positively life changing. The scientist and writer Carl Sagan, for instance, who was a driving force behind NASA's Viking Programme to put robot probes on Mars, found inspiration by reading Edgar Rice Burroughs' *Barsoom* adventures. These SF potboilers feature the heroic soldier of fortune John Carter, a fearless adventurer who travelled from Earth to Barsoom (Mars) simply by wishing very hard that he could be there. Sagan recounts (with no trace of embarrassment) how as a boy he used to stand out back of his house when Mars was high in the heavens, hold up his arms and wish very hard that he could go there. On 20 July 1976 the Viking 1 Lander set down on the Chryse Planitia plain and transmitted the first ground-level pictures of our nearest planetary neighbour – thus doubtless providing inspiration for future generations of scientists.

Incidentally, in 1975 Carl Sagan was awarded the Joseph Priestley Award for 'distinguished contributions to the welfare of Mankind' and in 1978 the Pulitzer Prize for literature. The benefits he gained from stories contributed in the end to the greater good of all.

> Edgar Rice Burroughs (1875–1950) was an American who began writing in his 30s. *A Princess of Mars* (1912) was the first of his highly successful Barsoom series, which ran to 11 volumes. Burroughs also created the character of Tarzan in *Tarzan of the Apes*, also in 1912. *The Science Fiction Source Book* (Ed. Wingrove, D. [1984] Harlow: Longman) notes that Burroughs' work appeals to the secret desires, dreams and illusions that draw readers so compulsively into such fantasy worlds. Ironically they led Carl Sagan to explore the reality behind the many fantastical notions of the Red Planet.

Sagan's story of being inspired by story is not uncommon, and in fact anyone can find hope, motivation, direction and strength by reading or being told about the lives of others, whether they are real people or 'just' figments of someone's imagination.

> 'First find out what your hero wants, then follow him.' Ray Bradbury

Ray Bradbury says this in the context of how to develop as a writer, but I think the point is equally applicable more generally in life. One of the world's great scholars and interpreters of mythology, Joseph Campbell[6] fears that young people today, and especially males, live in a *demythologized society*, one where great and ancient mythical stories are regarded as no more than superficial fantastical tales meant only for kids. And where the word 'myth' has become synonymous with 'untruth' or fiction, and where celebrities have taken the place of heroes.

Campbell maintains that the hero figure is one who makes sacrifices to benefit others while celebrities serve themselves. He argues forcefully that when a society is in spiritual crisis, through simple unbelief or unquestioning fundamentalist belief, then guidance in the form of mythical 'templates' and hero stories are like lifeblood. 'Maybe,' says Campbell, 'we need some hero who will give voice to our deeper longing' for spiritual values and connectedness to the world.

A note on inspiration

Sometimes children wonder what inspires writers. I always ask them what they mean by 'inspiration'. Usually they mean what gives me ideas for stories, but I take a little time to mention that inspiration is actually about *breathing*. The word comes from the Greek *inspirare*, 'to breathe upon'. It is the breath of life, the spirit that animates us. Inspiration is about breathing in experiences and breathing out our stories, what we think and how we feel about things. It is about appreciating what is wonderful ('wonder-full') and wanting to participate in that. Inspiration means being more fully alive in the world – connected to it and valuing our mortal life in the way that Campbell is suggesting.

WOW! – Worlds of Wonder

Professor of Education Kieran Egan[7] argues persuasively that as children grow they make sense of the world in a variety of ways through a layered development of understanding that quite early on in childhood displays the quality of myth. Mythic understanding arises from a young child's desire to find explanations in a world full of mystery and wonder. Young children mythologize – they create narratives, which anchor what they experience to some kind of reason. That these explanations are not true (as far as we know, and whatever the word 'true' means) doesn't make them any less useful. They are an aspect of every child's natural curiosity, that most precious of gifts which it is our duty, surely, to cultivate however we can.

Stories of all kinds feed the child's need to 'narratize the world', and support her as her intellectual abilities grow. Older children pass through a Romantic understanding (to use Egan's term) into an adult Philosophic understanding of how things might be. Romantic understanding is characterized still by a sense of wonder but a desire to find limits and boundaries; to create a 'fence of rationality' as it were so that we can locate ourselves in life and get our bearings. Stories as self-contained 'units of experience', and because they can be categorized in a number of ways, help here too.

Adult Philosophic understanding is, as the root of the word 'philosophy' suggests, based on wisdom and understanding. This is most usually expressed through language. As I've mentioned, we create frameworks of meaning which are both generated by words and expressed and explored with words. As adults we live in a world of words. And it is no great insight to point out that words can be used to persuade, manipulate and control our models of reality and thus our actions.

Refreshingly, and luckily, Kieran Egan argues that Philosophic understanding is not the end of the story. Many adults develop an ironic understanding whereby we refuse to take what we think we know as a given. Instead, we seek to test our maps and models in as many ways as our creativity can devise. We doubt, we question, we challenge, we demand further explanation and proof. In short, we will not be spun a yarn and allow it to lead us astray.

An important point to repeat is that Egan's 'hierarchy of understandings' is a layered thing. As adults we do not lose the ability to understand the world in earlier and more childlike ways. The writer Alan Garner has said that human beings are like onions, we have layers. What we are and can become depends on what has gone before. To be creatively curious adults we need to access the WOW-factor, the worlds of wonder, we enjoyed as children. And in story we have an infinity of wonderful worlds at our disposal.

> 'Curiosity is one of the most permanent and certain characteristics of a vigorous mind.' Samuel Johnson

The thinking skills link

Worlds of wonder and the pretend worlds found in stories often amount to the same thing. To wonder is one of our must basic and vital ways of thinking. 'I wonder' must be a phrase familiar to scientists, explorers, poets, technologists … The list is endless. What a tragedy it is if schools, obsessed with tests, targets and league tables fail to create opportunities for every child in every class every day to wonder about something.

Stories evoke wonder in the deepest sense of the word. They form the soil out of which symbolic thought can grow. Wonder strikes at the heart, while 'to wonder' as a verb means to seek explanations and reasons for the things we experience. As a storyteller I often witness audiences of children leaning forward with eyes wide (and sometimes mouths wide too), giving rapt attention as they lose themselves in a story. Few concentration problems here!

Afterwards the same children are full of questions – But why did/How come/Who could have known/What would have happened if … ? And this is a natural springboard into ways of thinking such as inference, speculation, assumption, deduction, observation, opinion (and its justification). Story sharing is so much more than children's passive listening, and something much more fruitful than dry, mechanical analysis. The philosopher Goethe suggested that anything that is dissected must first necessarily die. Exploring stories together in this way is not deconstruction but a *synthesis* of ideas, the creation of something more than there was before, because you were all there together in that experience.

Fifty years ago the educationalist Benjamin Bloom[8] devised a way of thinking about thinking. He called it a taxonomy of thinking skills, with knowledge and comprehension at the bottom of the 'ladder' and evaluation and synthesis at the top. It is worth noting that schools, in order to get children through tests, 'deliver' great quantities of knowledge and test their comprehension of it by having them parrot back the answers. I suspect that Bloom would not be satisfied with this state of affairs; nor am I, and nor are a growing number of teachers and parents.

This is not the place to discuss these complex and often contentions issues, save to say that when children are encouraged to wonder and ask questions about stories they are developing the kinds of powerful thinking mentioned above that can have a swift and direct impact on the quality of their understanding of the subjects they study at school.

Ways of doing – Story as strategy

Stories are pathways of potential. They are strategies that point towards different ground. Good stories explore desires and motivations, reasons and relationships, actions and consequences. Good stories suggest resolutions – 're-solutions' where old problems and dilemmas (but fresh to us perhaps) are solved again in ways we might not previously have imagined …

Some time ago I was helping a group of 10 year olds with their story writing, though I tend to call it story *making* since writing it down is only part of the process. First comes the inspiration and fragmentary ideas, then the trains of thought that will form the narrative. Josh, sitting by himself (voluntarily, for quietness) seemed to be struggling in these early stages. I asked him if he minded me sitting with him to read what notes he had made. Rather than a recognizable story Josh had scribbled what looked like snatches from a diary. He had written about being intimidated by a bigger boy in school and how he wanted just to get away from it all.

It was tempting to be concerned and ask him more about his circumstances, and perhaps suggest talking to his teacher or other adults at school … Tempting, and wrong, because he wanted to escape from the situation, not be looped back into it.

So I asked him instead that, if these were ideas for a story, what picture first came into his head. 'I'm driving away fast. I'm in a Mini. I like Minis', he said with a smile. I replied, 'So you're in your Mini and where are you going?' He frowned. 'I don't really know. Just away. And I'm looking in my rear view mirror now and there's a big truck coming up fast behind me. It's a juggernaut …' (It turned out later that Josh knew this word because of a character he'd seen in an X-Men film. Juggernaut smashed through walls and seemed unstoppable.)

I realized that Josh was still worrying about being bullied. 'Put your foot down,' I suggested. 'The juggernaut's got a bigger engine,' he countered. 'I can't shake him.' 'Is the truck trying to overtake you or run you off the road?' Josh shook his head. 'No, it's just that I have to keep going as fast as I can to stay ahead of him.' 'Maybe your Mini's like a red rag to a bull – Maybe the juggernaut driver is jealous of what you've got.' 'Maybe …' Josh said. 'Anyway, that's his problem. Look what's happening – You're zooming along so fast you're not really noticing the scenery, and you don't have any destination in mind. You're going nowhere fast!'

I didn't know if Josh realized the allegorical nature of what we were doing. Not that it mattered because he was just going along with the story-making game. He shrugged, accepting that trying to outspeed the juggernaut was pretty pointless. Then Josh said, 'I'll make a pit stop. I'll pull in for some fuel. There's a garage up ahead.' 'Good idea.'

And then I dared to say, 'Why not get a spray job on the Mini so it's not red any more? Maybe changing the colour will change the way people think about it.' Josh nodded. 'OK.'

So we pulled into the garage and a moment later the great juggernaut swerved off the road and thundered on to the forecourt with a scream of brakes and huge clouds of dust. 'Get out of the car Josh,' I advised him. 'You've got every right to be here.' 'He's getting out too, stepping down from his cab ...'

Then, completely unexpectedly, Josh smiled and chuckled. His eyes had been gazing into the distance, but now he looked at me. 'He's no bigger than I am! The juggernaut is huge but he's not. And he thought I was small because the Mini is small. But we're both the same size really!'

We rounded off the narrative with Josh saying good morning to the juggernaut driver, who more or less ignored him as he went into the nearby diner. Josh got his car resprayed a racing green and, as he drove away, saw that the juggernaut was still there parked on the forecourt, dwindling and becoming smaller in the rear view mirror.

It was clear that this ten-minute session of story making resolved something within Josh. Perhaps it did not settle the bullying situation (I never found out), but Josh's *perception* of it and the way he felt about it had changed. Changed perception usually results in changed behaviour. I feel certain that if Josh's manner shifted, the bully might well now leave him alone.

A great deal of work in the neurosciences in recent decades[9] reveals that at the level of brain cells we make no distinction between fantasy and reality. Our thoughts influence our feelings and physical responses in an endless feedback loop. That is the basis of worry, for example. Through the power of imagination we can conjure up some unpleasant scenario, either of something from the past that has already happened, or something that might occur in the future – *and react to it as though it were happening here and now.* Our reaction is real, and sometimes as strong as it would be if the unfortunate events were actually unfolding. There is a wise old saying that 'Worry is like being on a rocking horse. You put a lot of energy into it but it gets you nowhere.' In terms of story making the first thing our main character could do is dismount ...

This is not a frivolous idea. If riding a rocking horse is a metaphor for worry, then getting off is a metaphor for an alternative strategy to resolve the problem. Consciously the logical rational part of the mind might think this is 'only' an inconsequential little story, but at the level of the subconscious – the realm of the mind that thinks in symbol and which oversees the body's automatic functions – something significant has been suggested.

This is another reason why stories, and especially myths and legends, are powerful. They resonate with the deeper levels of the mind and, when their (sometimes consciously unrecognized) meanings are woven into the map of reality, people's perceptions and feelings and their very physiology can change. In recent years the notion of the *therapeutic metaphor* has been of growing importance in many fields of psychotherapy[10]. Increasingly the power of 'make believe' is being exploited for healing purposes. These days whenever I use the term make believe I think of it as *making beliefs*. To believe is – when we trace the roots of the word – to allow (from the Old English *lyfan*), and has links with the now-archaic term *lief*, meaning 'willingly'. Beliefs form the context of our lives; and I was fascinated to discover not long ago that the word 'context' (linked as it is with 'text') means 'to braid'. We braid meanings up out of life events and make beliefs from them, which affect not only how we look at the world but also how we respond within, perhaps (so some scientists claim) down to a cellular level.

'Words are a convenient way of pointing towards realities'. Charles T. Tart, Psychologist

Some years ago a young lady with a lack of self-confidence visited a hypnotherapist friend of mine. 'I know it's silly,' she complained, 'and I tell myself there's no need to feel so vulnerable and shy. I try very hard to feel confident and to put on a brave face ...'

'Maybe trying hard is not the best way to go about it then,' the therapist suggested, 'given that you still have the problem.'

'So what can I do!'

'Well, start by just settling yourself. Let your eyes close when you're ready and imagine a pleasant scene ... I'd be pleased to know a little bit about the place that you're thinking of ...'

The young lady smiled. 'It's my garden at home', she said. 'I love my garden.'

'And I wonder if, very soon now, you'll notice something there that has significance to the problem you will resolve ...'

There was a brief pause, then she frowned. 'Oh! There's a wall – there's a big tall brick wall in my garden! But I don't have one there really.'

'Never mind, this is only make believe after all ... So perhaps the significance of the wall will become clearer when you notice something else now – '

'There's a ball' she said at once. 'There's a football lying at my feet.'

'What do you want to do?'

'I'm going to kick that ball over the wall! ... But I can't. No matter how hard I kick it, it keeps hitting the wall and bouncing back to me.'

'Well we're in the wonderful world of imagination now, so notice what happens to help you with that ball ...'

She chuckled. 'It's grown wings! They're feathery white wings like a dove has.'

'And so, now?'

'Now the ball is flying over the wall when I kick it. There it goes!'

'That's good. Is there anything more that needs to happen now for you to have the greatest benefit from all this?'

'I'm going to *be* that ball', she said. 'I am the ball and I'm flying over the wall!'

At this point she stretched out her arms. She beamed with delight then opened her eyes, looked at the therapist and chuckled. 'So what was that about?' she wanted to know.

'I'm not sure', the therapist told her. 'But how do you feel?'

She felt fine, kind of excited, she said. The therapist asked her to call him in a week with a progress report. When the call came, the young lady said that she was much more confident now and couldn't understand why it had been such a problem before ...

This little story puts me in mind of a writing workshop session I once did. The children were asking questions and at one point one of the adults joined in too. She said, 'So what do you do, Steve, when you get writer's block and really hit a barrier?' 'Well,' I said, 'I put a doorway in it and walk through. Or maybe I could ... ?' I looked at the kids. 'Maybe you could fly over it with a jet-pack', said one boy. 'Or float over in a hot air balloon', said another. Trampolines, ladders, rockets, anti-gravity boots and giant birds were also suggested. Later on I took her aside and mentioned the potential danger in talking about writer's 'blocks' and 'barriers'. 'The children will pick up on that message and might build it into their beliefs about writing. Maybe it would help if that point where the words won't flow were called a writer's opportunity ...'

'There are two ways to live your life. One is as though nothing is a miracle. The other is as though everything is a miracle.' Albert Einstein

Incidentally the word 'miracle' comes from the Latin *mirari*, 'to wonder at'.

Long ago and far away (and here and now)

Stories are *integrative*. We not only incorporate them into our world view, but they in turn help us to be part of that world and, at best, to live as decent, useful, creative and fulfilled human beings.

One aspect of the unifying force of stories is known as 'The Ladder to the Moon'. This idea, which is part of the oral tradition of storytelling, uses the metaphor of the ladder with one end rooted in the soil and the other end lost among the stars. At ground level we have 'earthy' stories; jokes, gossip, hearsay – the kind of stuff you would talk about on the street or in your local corner shop or over your back garden fence. Such stories are the currency, the small change, of everyday interaction.

Further up the ladder we come to neighbourhood tales and family tales. These stories serve to widen our perspective to take in the importance of community and links of blood. They are reminders, if you will, that no one is an island. They are closely related to ancestor and history tales, which extend our appreciation back through time and allow us to realize that each of us has roots that go deep. These stories strengthen our sense of belonging and help us to honour those who have gone before us and passed on.

Stories of magic, fairy tales and legends engage our all-important sense of wonder, that energy by which the world is kept fresh and alive, as is our curiosity and the urge to find out more about it. Margaret Meek, who researches in education, calls such moments of sudden revelation *firstness* – that uplifting sense of original seeing which does not lead to dull familiarity but, rather, to a deeper excitement and admiration based on greater awareness. Stories of all kinds, but perhaps especially tales of enchantment, offer children and adults alike the 'peak experience' of firstness over and over again. As Margaret Meek also says, 'We do not only thrive on stories, we survive by telling and retelling them as history, discovery and invention'.

At the top of the ladder, with our heads in the heavens, we come to the great myths, sacred stories and creation tales that explore the deepest roots and purposes of our existence and point ahead to mysteries that may forever lie beyond our understanding. Here in their telling the ineffable and the numinous are connected to the soil. Our grandest and most searching questions are born of the same brains that relish hearing about some local scandal, or that find humour in the bawdy joke we hear down at the pub. The long tradition of story, its very nature, celebrates the fact that we are all human beings, all alive together now in this world, all searching for meaning and the answers to the questions that storm through our minds and which, ultimately, make us what we are.

> 'Life does not consist mainly, or even largely, of facts and happenings. It consists mainly of the storm of thoughts that is forever blowing through one's head.' Mark Twain

So far I have talked about why stories are important and I hope that you have been persuaded to agree. Perhaps what I have said will add to the reasons why you choose to share stories with your children. At the very least it is worth doing because, for that little time, you are partaking of something special together.

At this point let's summarize why stories matter.

- Sharing a story creates a quiet time where you and your children share a common experience. Stories form part of the 'glue' that binds and strengthens relationships. More generally, stories transmit wisdom and experience that is basic to all of humanity.

- Stories provide a rich field of ideas for imaginative exploration and discussion. Talking about stories and what they mean to us develops thinking and language.

- Travel broadens the mind ... Stories allow children mentally to visit distant times, places and people. They help us to appreciate what the world looks like from many different viewpoints. Stories open doorways to other cultures and encourage us to understand how different people feel. Stories deepen our empathy and widen our perceptions.

- Stories root the abstract in the concrete. They don't just tell; good stories *immerse* the reader or listener and engage the feelings as well as the mind. They put knowledge into a context and create a platform for insight and understanding. Stories are powerful teachers.

- Stories form a highly structured way of communicating ideas, knowledge, beliefs, attitudes and values. A story shows how a problem can be resolved.

- Stories help us to understand and rehearse rules, roles, rights and responsibilities. The characters in stories model ways of behaving and demonstrate that actions have consequences. Stories ask the question 'what if?' and show us some of the possible answers.

- Stories feed the imaginative play of young children. Play itself brings the experience of a story into the real world of the child and thus helps to develop their personality. For older children and for adults, stories can act as an inspiration which drives enquiry into different subject areas. Reading Science Fiction has inspired many scientists in their professional field, for instance. At all levels stories aid the construction of meaning.

- Stories can evoke a wide range of emotions in us as we participate in the lives of the characters. Stories create the opportunity for empathy, for us to be more fully feeling human beings.

- An old Eastern European proverb says 'The tools sharpen themselves.' Listening to stories allows children to gain insight into how narratives are constructed, which in turn helps their creative writing. Increasing confidence in handling language leads to benefits in other forms of writing. Enjoying stories boosts a child's linguistic intelligence.

- We can 'escape' into a story and forget our worries and cares. A story can thrill and excite us, make us feel (safely) scared, make us laugh, make us cry. But in most cases as we read or listen to a story we can *relax*.

'What shall we tell you? Tales, marvellous tales of ships and stars and isles where good men rest ...' (*Golden Journey to Samarkand* – James Elroy Flecker)

The world of the story

When I work with children I tell them about how my own interest in books and reading was kindled when as a boy I was given the first Dr Who story to be published in paperback. I was already watching the TV series (then starring William Hartnell as the Doctor), but the book as it were opened up a new dimension of enjoyment.

I tell children that I loved the idea of bundling into the Doctor's space-time vehicle, the TARDIS, which is much bigger on the inside than on the outside, and by pushing a few buttons could be transported to the most marvellous adventures *anywhere*. I then say how a good story is like the TARDIS; it's bigger on the inside than the outside and pushes the buttons of your imagination to take you adventuring wherever you choose to go.

But first we must open the doorway …

The wonderful storyteller Eileen Colwell[11] advises that the world of the story is created by an interaction between the teller, the listener(s) and the story itself. They all go into the mix. Before we can blend these ingredients successfully, I feel that some basic points need to be considered:

- Be clear why sharing stories with children is an important parenting skill.

- Do it out of love for your children rather than as a duty or a chore.

- Commit yourself to it. Once you introduce story time into your parenting it must be an ongoing thing. This means that it becomes a part of your life (something much more than a part of your routine).

- Establish the boundaries of the shared time. Make it 20 minutes each night, 30 minutes every other day – or whatever is most appropriate. Be firm in this, with yourself and with your children. When the time is up, end the session – though try to pace what you do so that it ends appropriately, at the end of a tale or with a cliffhanger.

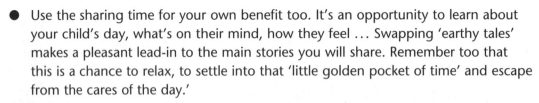

- Use the sharing time for your own benefit too. It's an opportunity to learn about your child's day, what's on their mind, how they feel … Swapping 'earthy tales' makes a pleasant lead-in to the main stories you will share. Remember too that this is a chance to relax, to settle into that 'little golden pocket of time' and escape from the cares of the day.'

Reading, telling and sharing

There is a big difference between reading, telling and sharing a story. Both reading and telling can form part of the sharing experience, though they do not amount to the same thing.

Reading is just that, offering the child the story verbatim as it is written by the author. It may be that that's exactly what you and your child would like. If you decide you'll read a tale, think about the following ...

- Choose a story that your child will like and ideally one that you do too. If *you* enjoy it you will read it more effectively. For all I have said about the educative nature of many stories, my advice is to avoid stories that you think are 'worthy' and/or that are included in the school curriculum – unless your child really *really* would like to have it read to her. Your aim is to build powerful and positive associations around story time, not to teach the classics or broaden your child's knowledge of authors and genres. That will occur anyway as another benefit of your story sharing commitment, but should not take precedence over simply enjoying story.

- Read the story through at least once to familiarize yourself with the plot. Have some sense of how long the reading will take, so that the story session is well rounded and can end – on time – at an appropriate point. This can sometimes mean not carrying on to the end of a chapter, but rather picking some suitable point mid-chapter to say 'And that's all for tonight.'

- Practise reading portions of it out loud. The storyteller Ruth Sawyer[12] advises that an 'easy, effortless flowing of words' makes the reading/telling a more enjoyable experience all round.

- When you read to the child, keep your voice well modulated (not overloud or too quiet, nor too shrill or 'over dramatic') and do not read too quickly. The story itself will suggest the pace. Tense and exciting scenes can be read at a faster pace than description or 'quiet' scenes, but remember the value of a dramatic pause and the pleasure to be had from savouring the sound of a well-constructed sentence.

- If the story's characters speak in dialect decide beforehand whether you will attempt those accents. Personally I think that you need to be very good at it to be at all convincing. Similarly if the characters have a 'cartoony' quality to their voices, practise first, decide whether you're good enough – and if you go ahead be consistent. There's nothing worse than sounding like Popeye one minute and Donald Duck the next.

- Your child might want to ask questions during the reading. At worst this can be a ploy to delay putting out the light! Usually though children sincerely want to know the answer. My tendency is to ask children to save up their questions for the end – too many interruptions break the flow of the reading and become distractions. Also, many of the questions will be answered later on in the story anyway. You could consider building a short question-and-answer or discussion slot into the overall story time.

- By the same token, avoid interrupting yourself to ask the child about what might happen next or why a character did such-and-such. It is not a comprehension exercise. When a child is lost in a story you will notice her gazing into space with rapt attention to the images flowing through her mind. This is the most wonderful mental state; it is true enchantment and a moment not to be broken.

● Where a story is illustrated, pick the moment when you will break off the reading to show a picture. Do not try to show the child a picture and keep reading at the same time as this will simply distract. In fact when you read the story to yourself initially you could even mark in the text where you will pause to show the illustrations. As appropriate you could chat about the pictures briefly, but not to the detriment of the child's and your enjoyment of the tale.

Talk about the pictures. Ask him to tell you about them.

Read with expression.

Choose a book you like -if you're enjoying it, your child probably will too.

Look at the front cover and the title. If it's a new book, you might discuss what you both think it's going to be about.

● However the stories you read are selected, you or your child might want to try other kinds of tales, authors, genres etc. Occasionally some portion of a story time can be devoted to talking about such things and even trying a 'sampling' session that can include extracts, poems, snippets of biography/autobiography – wherever your fancy takes you. You might even think of leading up to a sampling session by a visit to the library. Browsing is a good skill for any child to acquire, and librarians will usually have a good knowledge of their stock and can most likely recommend some titles.

● When is a child old enough for story times to end? Personally I think there is no upper limit and that people of all ages enjoy having stories read or told to them. How much better the world would be if families gathered at a regular set time to step through that doorway into other worlds ... Probably though there will come a time when your child says they are 'not a kid any more' and thinks themself too old for story time. You must of course respect that, but it might be worth suggesting that a) the time in future could be put by at least to chat or for some other shared activity or b) your child tells you a story, if not every night then occasionally, as a treat.

'Our society needs people with dreams.' Amit Goswami, The Self-Aware Universe

Storytelling

To my mind storytelling is a step beyond just reading one out. A tale to be told has been absorbed and assimilated by the teller: it has been taken into the storyteller and made their own. It may be a traditional story or folktale, a true experience of the storyteller's or someone else's. Perhaps it is a story that you'll invent just for your child, made up in segments day by day or even (though this takes quick wits as well as a good imagination) created on the spur of the moment to satisfy her craving to 'tell me more!' Lewis Carroll is one author who did this: another is Rudyard Kipling who made up his *Just So Stories* for his 'best beloved' daughter Josephine. However it is done, a story-to-be-told is something quite unique, a treasure that brings special delight to the listener as much as it does to the teller. 'My father told me the following story when I was a child.'

'Coal mining in South Wales was never the safest of occupations. But back then when I was a boy in the 1930s accidents were not rare and when the colliers went off to work there was always that shadow in the minds of the womenfolk that maybe they would not be coming back.

Well this particular evening Beattie Isaacs was standing in Dave Williams' shop. She'd just popped out of the house to pick up a few last minute groceries, onions actually. Her husband Dai was due off-shift in an hour or so and she had decided to cook him a couple of lamb chops. And Dai loved plenty of onions in his gravy. It was October and already dark outside even by half-past five. The wind was cold and carried a few speckles of rain mixed in with the blowing leaves. The forecast on the radio earlier had not been good.

Beattie bought her onions and was just exchanging a few words with Lena Butler near the door when Nigel Lloyd burst in almost screaming – "There's been a tunnel collapse down the pit! A collapse – men trapped! A collapse!" His hair was all awry and his clothes a mess. He was a scraggy kid anyway – well the Lloyd family was a bit like that, you know ... And his eyes were wide as saucers and his face had a stunned look. Then he was gone, off up the street, as though the wind had snatched him away.

The blood drained out of Beattie's face and Lena Butler had to hold her up. She dropped the bag of onions and one rolled away under the apple box (and you can be sure Dave

Williams found it there and sold it again to another customer!) "Oh my God", Beattie whispered, "Oh my God, my Dai is on that shift ..."

There was no way that Lena could make the situation sound more hopeful. Everyone in the valleys lived with the possibility of such a terrible accident. It had happened before, all through the Rhonddas. Many families had been touched by it.

Well anyway. Lena was a good friend and she took Beattie home and made her a strong sweet cup of tea, then sent her son Neil down to the colliery to find out the news. He was back an hour later with not much to tell. A rescue team had gone down there – this was in B shaft – and the only word coming out was that the collapse was a bad one, very bad.

Lena stayed until gone eight, but then Beattie told her to go home because her own cousin's husband was a miner too, on the same shift as Dai, and it was only right that she should be there for them.

Can you imagine how the shadows of gloomy despair gathered in that house as Beattie sat alone, nursing her empty tea cup, hunched forward in her chair by the fire, braving that awful fear? She sat like this for another hour and another 30 minutes after that ... And then she heard a familiar clumping of boots outside on the pavement and a scuff at the doorstep. A shock went through her heart and she jumped up and hurried into the hallway ...

There was a streetlamp just opposite and Beattie saw the silhouette of her man through the frosted-coloured glass of the front door. He was a shadow haloed in curls of light. She dragged the door open and there was her Dai, pale as death beneath the coal dust smudged on his face, and his eyes big with horror. "I only came to say I love you, Beatrice my darling. And you'll be all right ... Now I must go and try to help the other men down there. I do love you ..."

And he turned and walked away up that quiet street, his broad back bent against the rain. She watched him go and she knew what it meant. And she was not surprised when, in the early hours, in that darkest time of the night, Terry Langford from the Miners' Union called by to say that he was so sorry, but they had found Dai Isaacs' body down that shaft. There had been no hope for him. He had been buried under ten tons of coal.'

My father told me that story when I was a boy, at just the age of innocence when a chilling tale lived up to its name as I listened. As I think of it I can still see Dai Isaacs' silhouette wreathed in light through the front-door glass, and feel the dread anticipation of knowing what had become of him – and what he was now! And I remember asking then 'Is it true Dad? Is it true?' And my father said, 'Well you ask any of the older people around here and they'll tell you ...' Which was no answer at all, but one which satisfied me then.

This is a story for children of perhaps 8 years old and upwards, but we can still learn some 'tricks of the telling' that help us to prepare stories for children outside that age range.

- Keep things as simple as possible, but no simpler. This is something that Albert Einstein advised when expounding scientific theories, but it's a good tip for storytellers too.

- Set the scene quickly and move on. In this case there are the bare facts of time and place, followed by the idea that accidents were common in the mines; this 'primes' the listener's anticipation for what is to follow. It's a good idea to do this, to drop a hint of what the story will be about.

- The story has to be believable. In fact scary tales, Fantasy stories, Science Fiction tales, etc., are all the more effective when the listener can believe in them. In this case one important aspect is that the people and places are so *ordinary*. The 'chill factor' is increased by the build-up being set in everyday circumstances. Stories of this kind often work better when the extraordinary grows out of the mundane.

See for example Garner, Alan (1972), *The Weirdstone of Brisingamen* (London: Collins), which is set around Alderley Edge in Cheshire; (1972) *Elidor* (Harmondsworth, Middlesex: Penguin Books), set in Manchester; Gordon, John (1984), *The Giant Under the Snow* (Harmondsworth, Middlesex: Puffin, Penguin Books), based in and around Norwich. An important aspect of the power of these and similar stories is the ordinariness and realism of the locations.

- The use of *particular details* helps in this too. This is a powerful thing to include in any story. The fact that Dai Isaacs likes plenty of onions in his gravy makes him more of a person to us, while the suspicion that Dave Williams the shop owner retrieved the onion that rolled away and sold it again later lifts him above being just a name. Adding a couple more details of the weather helps to establish the mood, while the snippet of gossip about the Lloyd family raises a smile perhaps and contrasts with and so highlights the horror of Nigel's awful news. Vivid little details add to the story's realism and serve in place of longer descriptions which slow the narrative.

- The 'drama' is carefully controlled. The whole story is quite low key (and this would be reflected in the tone of the teller's voice). Nigel Lloyd's appearance at the shop marks the only 'loudly dramatic' point, but even then in the telling I wouldn't shout out Nigel's words. You might think too – imagining yourself telling this tale – where and how you might make dramatic pauses and silences work for you.

- Think about what to leave out. Eastern philosophy says that the beauty of a wheel is due as much to the spaces between the spokes as to the spokes themselves, while the usefulness of a cup lies in the emptiness that the porcelain contains. In this story notice how the word 'ghost' is not mentioned at all, while the descriptive details as

Dai Isaacs stands at the door are minimal – and certainly should not be overdone. I would say as a general rule that a story works better if it is short and sparse rather than being lengthened through too much description and a glut of details.

Story sharing with younger children

Just about all of the principles and some of the techniques already mentioned apply when story sharing with young children (babies and toddlers up to around age 5). However here are some extra ideas and tips that you might find useful with this particular age range.

- With babies and toddlers begin by not attempting to tell a story at all. Take suitable colourful pictures from magazines and or use photographs and explore these with your child. Talk with her about the lovely bright colours, the shapes, what people and animals, etc., might be doing.

- Make up (or research beforehand) rhymes and songs around a particular picture. For example if you use a photo of a cat sing familiar songs like 'Pussycat pussycat where have you been' / 'Ding dong bell a pussy's in the well'.

- Make up 'mini adventures' using a child's favourite toys. Using a toy cat for instance hide the cat and ask 'Where has the cat gone?' Put the same wonder and excitement into your voice that will match how the child feels. Make the cat pop back into view and say 'Here she is! But when will she go away next?' And so on. This can easily grow into a game of peek-a-boo, which surely all little children love.

- Progress to narratives that are slightly more elaborate (but still relatively simple). Using a cat picture say 'What sounds does a cat make?' Demonstrate meowing and purring and encourage your child to join in. Again talk about the colours of the cat, the softness of its fur, etc. This is a good opportunity to talk about and teach names, colours, sounds and textures.

- Shop-bought rag books and foam books (for use at bath time!) are much more common these days. Use these by all means but take care that children don't transfer the habit of bending, chewing and scrunching up such books to paper books. Teach good book handling habits from the outset. Board books are also easily available. Let young children handle these as you teach careful and respectful handling. When you share books like this with children, don't just read the words, be prepared to *elaborate* and *improvise*. These are two important skills which you are modelling for your children also to acquire. Younger children often like to hear their favourite stories again and again. Indulge this wish certainly, but insist that sometimes you want to change the story a bit; the ending maybe or by adding extra adventures to the main plot. The creativity that you bring to bear in playing with such stories will transfer to the children and add a different kind of delight to story time.

● There are now available board books with inserts of objects and characters that can be removed and fitted into place in different ways on different pages, and that can also be used independently to create story sequences that you and your children can elaborate upon. This adds a wonderful element of interactivity to your story sharing and serves as a beneficial device for developing the skills of memory and figuring out what happens next.

● When you feel the time is right move to more complex stories, which practically will still amount to picture books with perhaps ten words maximum on a page. Often the plots in such books are either non-existent or very simple. Again it's a matter of exploring the pictures and simple written descriptions and being careful not to overwhelm a child and dampen her delight with too much information. Sometimes picture books come with a soft toy of one or more of the characters. Use them to bring the 'story' more to life and create new adventures of your own.

● Usually by age 3+ children can cope with – and indeed sometimes demand – more complex books. These will probably still be picture books but of greater complexity. And again the emphasis is on you telling the stories rather than reading verbatim. As and when you re-read these tales, ask your children to identify some key words, character names, etc. In other words introduce and reinforce the vital skill of matching letter patterns with sounds and meanings. Your own judgement about what your child can cope with will most likely serve you well, but in any case be sensitive to 'information overwhelm'. Keep it simple – say

'This is the letter b and look, here it is in baby, ball', and so on. Point out things in the room that start with that letter.

● At some point you might want to introduce your child to fairy tales. There are many wonderful picture book adaptations and, for rather older children, many fine collections are available. One series I wholeheartedly recommend is published by Ladybird. These little books feature a colourful picture alternating with a page of text. The books are readily and inexpensively available through online bookstores such as Amazon. Key in *Ladybird Tales* and see what happens.

It is important to stress that when sharing stories with children of any age you must use stories that you are familiar with yourself – and that you enjoy. Every tip and technique I can offer you will be all the more effective given your own enthusiasm.

Practice run

I wonder if you'd take some time to work on your storytelling skills by using the tale of the mining disaster that you read earlier? Try these things ...

● Firstly read the story out loud just to get the feel of it 'in your mouth'. At this stage is there anything you'd want to change – any words you'd care to replace or (just one or two) details you'd like to add?

● Read it aloud again, this time recording it. Then play it back (yes I know, I don't like the sound of my voice on tape either). Notice especially the pace of the reading; whether you are rushing at all, for instance. And be aware of the tone and inflexion of your voice. Remember that trying to force humour or 'chill', tension or wonder through over-dramatizing with the voice will not work. More subtle inflexions and nuances of tone work best.

● Study the structure of the story itself. Jot down very briefly the job that each paragraph does. Note any vivid details that appeal to you and/or which 'lift' the story and make it more memorable. Again, is there anything you would add, leave out or change to make the story your own?

● Now try telling the story aloud. You don't need an audience. Have your notes with you, but refer to them as little as possible. During the telling, notice what's going on in your head. The most powerful tellings happen when the teller, in creating the world of the story for his listeners, *experiences* that world for him or herself in all of its sensory richness. See the characters, feel the cold October wind, smell that 'grocery' smell inside Dave Williams's shop, hear the small thud of the onion as it drops to the floor and rolls away, *become* Beattie Isaacs as she stands in a darkened hallway looking at that frosted silhouette through the glass panel of the front door ...

This last point is very important. The ability to visualize the story as you speak it is crucial to the success of the telling. And by 'visualize' I mean being aware of it in your imagination using all of your senses. In that way you relive the story each time you tell it, and in so doing bring it alive for your listeners.

Incidentally, using stories is a great way of helping your children to develop their own ability to visualize. This mental skill is one aspect of what is called *metacognition* – noticing and directing the thoughts passing through our own minds. It is in my view the basis for developing all other kinds of thinking and so is fundamental to any child's education.

> Metacognitive children don't just notice what they think but also *how* they are thinking and why. This kind of inner awareness helps children to choose particular thinking 'tools' appropriately and for a range of purposes.

When you feel confident that you have 'absorbed' the story, try it out on someone. If the example we've used isn't suitable for your own child then find another willing listener. The tale doesn't take long to tell, and it is important that you boost your confidence and 'ease of telling' through practice.

Once this stage is reached, you can go through the process of developing a story-to-tell with just about any tale that you choose. The storyteller Ruth Sawyer however, who I mentioned earlier, feels strongly that learning by experiment and experience is by far preferable to learning by rule-of-thumb direction. With that in mind, take what bits of advice I've given that you find relevant, make them your own, and do not be afraid to discard what's left.

Ruth Sawyer also says that 'words are our clay', so now be bold and get your hands dirty as you shape stories for the telling.

> 'In so many forms of entertainment today you simply sit back and things are done to you or for you. But in storytelling the listener is very actively involved creating images from the words … Both are conjuring up all those mind pictures and the story comes alive.'
> Connie Regan (Renowned American storyteller)

Going beyond the given

Occasionally I am asked to tell stories in places other than schools. Some years ago the librarian at a high security prison wondered if I'd do some storytelling to an invited audience of inmates. With a great deal of trepidation I accepted and a couple of weeks later found myself in the prison library facing around 20 men, one of whom was a huge body-building type with shaved head, tattoos and a gold (upper-right canine) tooth. This man sat with his legs out, ankles crossed, arms folded, completely unresponsive for the first half hour or so ...

Then I told the story, which I had written years before, of a man who inherits the unusual gift that, whatever damage is done to him, that damage turns back upon the perpetrator. If someone hits the man, the assailant feels the pain. If someone tries to rob him, the thief finds he loses out somehow himself. When society finds out about this man, they try in ever more violent ways to destroy him, with terrible consequences.

This is not a children's story of course, but the point is that as I told it the inmate with the gold tooth started to pay more attention. His eyes became more animated. He unfolded his arms and ended up leaning forward in his chair listening with rapt attention to every word. When I finished he said, very quietly, 'That story you just told, is it true?' And no one dared to laugh at him. I didn't appreciate at the time that I might have put myself in a dangerous situation, but luckily I had the presence of mind to say 'Like all good stories, this one tells you something true ...'

The huge man fixed me with his eyes a moment longer, smiled with a glint of gold tooth, then sat back and folded his arms again. My answer had satisfied him and I lived to tell that story another day.

Stories can work on many levels. We may simply enjoy a tale for its entertainment value, perhaps consciously appreciating the cleverness of the plot, the vividness of descriptive passages or the quirkiness of a character. But even as our conscious attention notices and values these things, we also assimilate the story on a subconscious level, draw meaning from it that we then incorporate into the way we look at the world. In other words it may exert an influence on our values, beliefs and attitudes.

This subject is too big to explore in so short a chapter, but it is worth noting that when we share stories with our children we are actually doing more than entertaining. We may be offering powerful 'messages' that children might not at the time be able to articulate or understand, but which nonetheless can affect them.

This is why I think it is important for children to be exposed to myths and legends, not just the magnificent stories from Egypt, Greece and Rome but from all cultures. Such tales 'polished like pebbles in the ocean of people's imaginations' can bring wisdom to young minds and suggest possibilities (usually through metaphor) for future contemplation, conduct and action.

Consider for instance the tale of the Athenian hero Theseus who, during his adventures, wanted to slay the dreaded Minotaur, half bull, half man, that dwelt within the Labyrinth. King Minos's daughter Ariadne fell in love with Theseus and so she gave him a ball of thread that he could use to trace his path through the maze and find his way out of it again. This is just what Theseus did, and so the 'Ariadne thread' conveys to us the insight that there is always a way out and the means to find it.

There are many wonderful collections of myths and legends written especially for children. Use the internet, your local library or a good bookshop to seek them out. If the age range of the stories doesn't suit your purposes, have a go at adapting them for retelling using the methods we've already explored.

Discussing the stories you share

I have already made the point that what counts most is the experience itself of sharing stories between yourself and your children, with all its attendant benefits. Personally I feel there is little need in this context to analyse or 'deconstruct' the stories, nor actually do I think there should too much explanation of them afterwards. Careful selection of stories before they are read or told will help to ensure that they are not beyond your child's understanding. Where they are puzzled or confused and full of questions your reply of 'Well what do you think about that?' will be of greater value than simply supplying 'the right answer'. Exploring possibilities encourages your child to use their imagination actively and to think things out for herself. This is a useful precursor to the creative approach that she can later bring to the ideas she encounters at school.

That said, there are lots of ways of creatively discussing the stories you share that will also develop your child's critical and analytical abilities. Here are some suggestions.

1. Spend some time comparing stories, ones by the same author perhaps, or written within the same genre. What makes a story a Fantasy story? What defines a Romance? Why was a certain character memorable? Which story did you like best and why? Explore why the authors constructed their stories as they did. Assume that everything an author does has a reason behind it, but feel free to have your own ideas and opinions as you explore.

2. Ask 'what if' type questions. What if a certain character had acted differently at a particular point? What if the author had written the story for younger children, how would it be different? What if there were a sequel, how might it carry on the story?

3. Make up more stories out of the stories you've read. Use the same themes, characters and even settings to weave new plots. Or try 'mix and match' type experiments. What if a character from one story met a character from another story? What might a conversation between them be like? If they were involved in a certain situation (choose one) how do you think they would react?

4. Ask your child if they would like to tell *you* a story sometimes. My own experience is that younger children especially love to be involved in this way. The tendency is for some children to interrupt and jump in with 'Something like that happened to

me once', so there must be an agreement that either your child has the whole of the telling time, or that they can tell their tale once you have finished yours.

5. Keep a reading log of the stories you share, featuring a brief outline of the story and what you thought of it. A friend of mine has created a 'story wall' with his children. This is a large cork notice board filled with the children's pictures of characters and scenes, book covers (copies of actual covers plus ones the kids have made up), memorable quotes from the tales, made up blurbs, etc.

6. Consider liaisons with your child's school. One school I know runs a story-sharing club where, once a week, some time is set aside for children to talk about the stories they've read (or had read to them) at home. Parents are invited in and there is even an occasional newsletter of recommended reading, news and views, quotes, etc. Your local library might also be prepared to run something similar.

All of these things reinforce in your child's mind the value you place on being with her. Time, love and attention are the three most important things that any parent can give. As someone once said, life is not a rehearsal. Childhood, 'that time when imagination is warm and impressions are permanent', only happens once. It is the foundation on which our adult lives are built. These quiet hours when you explore the magical world of story together will be loved and remembered forever.

'Abracadabra' – (Aramaic) 'I create as I speak'

Footnotes and further reading

1. Postman, N. and Weingartner, C. (1972), *Teaching as a Subversive Activity*. Harmondsworth: Penguin.

2. Carl Sagan (1934–96) was a noted visionary and scientist in the fields of biology and astrophysics. His 1980 TV series *Cosmos* set new standards in how the wonders of the universe were communicated to the general public. Source of quote – www.brainyquote.com.

3. Palmer, Sue (2006), *Toxic Childhood: How the Modern World is Damaging Our Children and What We Can Do About it*. London: Orion.

4. Abbott, J. and Ryan, T. (2000), *The Unfinished Revolution: Learning, Human Behaviour, Community and Political Paradox*. Stafford: Network Educational Press, 'Visions of Education' series.

5. The sourcebook for much of the understanding of and discussion about people's ability to understand the world in different ways (through the 'natural intelligences') is Gardner, Howard (1993), *Multiple Intelligences: The Theory in Practice*. New York: Basic Books.

6. Joseph Campbell (1904–87) was an American professor and writer in the fields of comparative religion and mythology. His seminal work is *The Hero with a Thousand*

Faces (1949) though he is also highly regarded for his massive four-volume work *The Masks of God*. His later commentaries on the power and purpose of myths as a living force in human society and the human psyche include *The Power of Myth* (with Bill Moyers) (1988), New York: Doubleday and *The Way of Myth* (with Fraser Boa) [1994], Boston & London: Shambala.

7.   Kieran Egan is Professor of Education at the Simon Fraser University and in 1991 won the Grawemeyer Award for Education. He has made intensive studies of the way in which understanding develops through childhood (see *The Educated Mind* (1997), Chicago: University of Chicago Press) and how the use of narrative structure and active imagination aid learning (see *Teaching as Story Telling* (1986), Chicago: University of Chicago Press and *Imagination in Teaching and Learning* (1992), London: Routledge).

8.   Bloom, B. (1958), *The Taxonomy of Educational Objectives*. London: Longman.

9.   For example the work of Ernest Lawrence Rossi (1993) in *The Psychobiology of Mind-Body Healing*. New York and London: W. W. Norton & Co.

10. See for example Berman, M. and Brown, D. (2002), *The Power Of Metaphor: Story Telling & Guided Journeys For Teachers, Trainers And Therapists*. Bancyfelin, Carmarthen: CrownHouse/Wallas; Wallas, Lee (1985), *Stories for the Third Ear*. New York and London: W.W. Norton & Co; Williams, Pat (1998), *How Stories Heal* (audio lecture). Chalvington, East Sussex: ETSI (European Therapy Studies Institute).

11. Colwell, Eileen (1980), *Storytelling*. London: The Bodley Head. Eileen Colwell also said that 'There are no frontiers in the world of stories.'

12. Sawyer, Ruth (1942 [1990]), *The Way of the Storyteller*. London: Penguin Books.

Introducing Tim Harding – *by Jim Houghton*

I first met Tim when he was a headteacher of an exciting primary school in North Lincolnshire. Bridget Gibbs, our editor and present convenor of the group, and I went to a performance of *That's Maths!*, which was a whole-school end of term production written, composed and orchestrated by Tim. The performing musicians were Tim's family and the cast was a substantial number of the children at the school. It was a superb spectacle but difficult to describe as it is much better to see and listen to it. The songs were full of fun and wit, yet reinforcing the learning objectives for Key Stage 2 Mathematics! The musical genres were rich and varied, ranging from Country and Western to Music Hall, and the whole performance was clearly a tremendous hit with all the assembled parents and carers. In fact, this led to NEP publishing a number of subject-based books/CDs all written and orchestrated by Tim but performed by the Harding family musicians. These informative and musically inspiring productions are, I'm pleased to say, still available from the present publishers of this book.

I also had the privilege of meeting the Harding family at their home and can only record that although very different individuals, Emily, Charlotte, Eleanor, Amanda and Tim all share and enjoy their music. The medium of music really has been for them a way of developing Tim's 3 Cs of Communication, Collaboration and Creativity which has clearly given them strength and cohesion as a family.

In this chapter Tim argues that music is also something innate that can either wither away or be nurtured into a developing skill and source of enjoyment for many children. He identifies a wide range of strategies to help children to develop their musical skills and talents and to maintain them through the teenage years into a lifelong source of satisfaction and joy. Just as in Steve's chapter on stories, Tim makes a strong argument for making, listening to and sharing music with your family, and offers a wealth of advice on how to encourage and support this process. The Harding family band is a powerful role model for where these simple ideas can lead and, by the way, are well worth listening to, should you ever have the opportunity!

chapter three

The family that plays together: The joy of making music

This chapter examines aspects of parenting from a musical perspective. It considers the benefits of involving children in making music, explores the wider issues of family music making, and suggests ways in which musical activities can be encouraged within the family. The final section uses music as both an illustration of and a metaphor for family life.

It aims to raise and explore issues and offer some opinions and suggestions which will hopefully stimulate both thought and discussion (fundamental aspects of successful family life) and creativity – including music making!

Prelude

Above all this chapter is about working together with your children. Spending time with them, connecting with them and building working relationships with them through engaging in creative and constructive activities together. Helping to shape the adults they will become, and developing skills, attitudes and abilities that will enrich their lives and equip them for the future. Encouraging them to develop individual skills within an interpersonal context as well as interpersonal skills themselves. In an age of increasing individual/screen interaction, it is vital that we retain activities which involve human contact. Of course technological development should be embraced, but as a society, we diminish the ability to relate to and work alongside others at our peril.

The family is an excellent place to start learning these skills. We all need our own space, our own interests, and contact with wider social groups; but interests fostered at home, with the right amounts of encouragement, can nurture both the area of interest and the system of values which lies behind it. And at the same time shared achievement creates bonds of trust, respect and self-worth.

As our children grow up this home-based interaction will extend to wider social groups – at schools and colleges, amongst peer and friendship groups and in the world of work. This need not however necessarily be at the expense of the family network: continuing family support and interaction is a stabilizing and educating factor that is too easily dismissed as individuals seek their independence.

Being a family

As we begin the twenty-first century, the very term 'family' encompasses a wide variety of social structures, from the OED definition of 'a group consisting of two parents and their children living together as a unit', to the single-parent family, the families containing step-parents or guardians and families with same-sex couples. Whatever the structure however, we all bring to the concept of family our own beliefs, values, aspirations, interests and opinions, as well as the experiences of our own family life which shaped these.

As parents who want the 'best' for our children, we are constantly striving to develop a good balance of self and social capability and responsibility in our children. But the dilemmas of parenthood are ever-present. Are we over- or under-protecting? Are we directing and shaping without dictating or suffocating? Are we encouraging or over-encouraging our children? Is what we want for them what they want? Are we providing guidance, without strangling their personal aspirations? Do they know what they want?

And because we all have different circumstances and personalities, the golden rule of parenting is that there is no golden rule! What will work for one family, parent or child, will not necessarily suit another. For example, while this chapter is about the positives of encouraging families to play music together, it may be that a child chooses to follow musical interests because they want to establish their own independent identity by pursuing a skill that no-one else in their family has mastered.

Furthermore, all these parenting dilemmas are set against the background of a twenty-first-century western social climate which is increasingly seen as deteriorating. The fragmenting of authority, respect and social codes, alongside the excesses of our modern culture put strains and stresses on the family unit – and particularly our children who can easily fall into the 'toxic childhood' so graphically identified by Sue Palmer in her recent book.[1]

Music

This chapter is about music because that is where my own – and my family's interests – mainly lie. However, engaging in sports, games, other creative arts and other interests will hold many of the same benefits in terms of co-operation and collaboration and may be equally valid, depending on you and your family. For me however, musical activities provide the perfect avenue for family interaction, encompassing as they do the 'three Cs' of character development:

- Communication
- Collaboration
- Creativity.

In addition to this it is emotionally satisfying; producing not only hopefully a result that is good to listen to, but also a sense of both personal and shared achievement – with enjoyable experiences along the way. Music is also an activity which is unrestricted by age and can be enjoyed at many different levels. All too many books about family music making restrict their activities to the early years – with an almost unwritten rule that once children are old enough to learn 'real' instruments at school, the involvement of the family is no longer important, and is relegated to a supporting role.

I would challenge this. Continued musical interaction will lead to continued communication within the family; and as individuals change and develop, roles, responsibilities and relationships will also change and develop.

The benefits to all members of the family will be great – working towards a common purpose builds relationships and mutual understanding. You learn to talk through differences of opinion in a secure environment which is underpinned by a sense of responsibility to and for each other, as well as sensitivity and mutual respect. To continue Sue Palmer's analogy – music can be one of the anti-toxins of family life.

I've got the music in me ... pass it on!

Surrounded by music: Stirring the emotions, inspiring the soul

The power of music should not be underestimated. It is the neural triathlon, triggering an incredible concatenation of neural events, along with many parallel processes. The incredible, linguistic, emotional, rhythmic, mnemonic powers of music have been a great source of entertainment and functionality in both our modern and ancient human environments.[2]

Music surrounds us: on television and radio, in the muzak of shops, in homes and public places. In this digital age we have unprecedented access to music. From the earphones of the iPod and mp3 player, to the massive speaker stacks of outdoor festivals, we have an ever-increasing ability to select the music we choose to listen to, as we create the personal soundtrack to our lives.

Indeed, music has a power over our lives. Songs and tunes can trigger thoughts and images in our long-term memories. The song that you first danced to with your partner can become the talisman of your relationship. An overheard snatch of a tune can suddenly resurrect memories of another time and place. We cannot stop the associations: music can be a great facilitator of memory.

Music can also capture and affect our moods. It can motivate and inspire, soothe or calm, help us to relax and reflect, irritate or please and sometimes even make us cry. It stirs our emotions and affects our feelings. A fast song can make the heart beat faster, while a slower paced song can make the heart rate slow down. Fast driving music, whether it be a rousing orchestral piece such as the final section of the 'William Tell Overture', a military march, or a heavy rock song, can raise our pulse, excite and energise us. It is no coincidence that this type of music is played at sporting events such as football or boxing matches as the players emerge. The motivating power of music fills us with positive feelings, and increased enthusiasm. Similarly, calm music can help us to concentrate and focus our thoughts. Contemplative music, which encourages reflection and spirituality, has long been a part of religious services and gatherings as well as being used for de-stressing activities.

Much of the music used to affect our mood is instrumental and evokes images, places and feelings through our imagination or memory. However, when music is combined with words, a symbiotic relationship is produced, which gives the whole a powerfully enhanced effect. Because song lyrics are concise, and often in short lines, with patterned linguistic devices such as alliteration, rhyme and rhythm, they are particularly memorable. During author discussions for this book, the words of an appropriate song were mentioned and recalled. As we listened to the lyrics of On Children[3] we agreed that the song encapsulates our feelings about the transient nature and responsibilities of parenthood. And listening to the recording of this song by the a cappella group, Sweet Honey in the Rock, the poignancy of the words is enhanced by a haunting tune skilfully sung with depth of emotion and feeling. Such music captures a mood – a sentiment – and becomes an experience that seems able to touch our very souls.

Give it a go

The greatest benefits can be drawn from active music making rather than passive listening activities.[4]

'Anyone can take up music. There are few activities that are more accessible and more rewarding. Yet it's a mind-boggling combination of physical co-ordination, intellectual and expressive activity.'[5]

It is not just listening to music that is beneficial to our development: taking part in music making can promote our intellectual, spiritual and even physical wellbeing. And the satisfaction and sense of achievement of performing a piece of music – at many different levels – can be immense.

As already referred to by Steve in the previous chapter, Sue Palmer in her book *Toxic Childhood* outlines three key abilities which help set children on the path to becoming well-balanced, useful and creative members of society: maintaining attention, deferring gratification and balancing your own needs against the needs of others.[6] Making music together fulfils all of these in abundance.

For example, learning to play a musical instrument can well be a long process. It requires patience, application and sustained attention. The initial results may not be very satisfying, but with time and perseverance, the excitement of creating recognisable and pleasurable sounds will be its own encouragement.

Unfortunately, in a world which increasingly rewards success instantly, many children don't get beyond the initial process of skill learning to experience the rewards. However, sustained application need not be seen purely as an individual chore. The traditional view of a child being shut in a room and not allowed to do anything else until they had done 30 minutes of piano/violin practice is a depressing one and all of us may know of someone who has been completely put off playing music in this way.

A University of East London study of 257 children showed that children who maintained interest in playing an instrument had started learning at an early age with a great deal of parental support and teachers who were friendly but not too technically able. It followed up the progress of 20 musically successful children and eight years later found that the most successful musicians had teachers who were 'not too pushy' but 'not too relaxed'. While a substantial amount of practice was needed, the most successful adult performers were not those who did the most practice, but those who took part in more concert activities as children, did lots of improvised music making, and who had mothers at home during their early years.[7]

Of course some individual study is required to master an instrument, but this may or may not be best done in an individual context and the answer is to achieve an appropriate balance that combines individual practice with group interaction. Practising with the right attitudes (combining reading music with improvisation and impromptu playing) has the additional benefit of being great fun. It is a good combination of endeavour and enthusiasm which can set a child in good stead for the future.

Eventually, through application will come the deferred gratification. The thrill of performance, particularly when others are involved, can be immense. So too for those who create music; the buzz of hearing your composition played for the first time can be intensely rewarding.

Finally, because music is essentially a social activity, it is best experienced together. Sometimes that can even just mean being part of a group listening to music together. But more often than not it involves making our own contribution sympathetically within the context of a group situation. Whether we are making music in a group of 50 or just two, it will require a level of participation where we have to balance our own needs against the needs of others.

Music in the womb

'Everybody is born musical: babies absorb music before they are even born ... Music is in our genes!'[8]

In his excellent book *Music Makes Your Child Smarter*, Philip Sheppard describes in some detail the innate musicality of all children, stating that 'We are all musical'. I often wonder if our first daughter's considerable rhythmic and drumming capabilities were determined by the fact that during pregnancy my wife played the violin in a folk-rock band – standing next to the drums! And as a 2-week-old baby she turned to stare with what I am sure was a look of recognition as my wife played her violin.

Most of us start life with a basic sense of rhythm, perhaps linked to our body systems. Our hearts beat to a steady pulse. And when we learn to walk, skip and run, we tend to do so to a regular beat. As we listen to the pattern of repeated sounds created by these activities, we can perhaps recognize the common rhythms that form the basis of the most popular musical forms.

To a greater or lesser extent therefore, we can all respond to music in a variety of forms.

But why are some people more musical than others?

Music and children – nature or nurture?

How often have you heard the proud parent after a school concert loudly declaring: 'I don't know how he/she is so good at that, he certainly doesn't get it from me!'

And yet it is generally agreed that we are all born with a modicum of musical/rhythmic talent. However some people seem to have specific musical skills over and above others. One such example is that of perfect pitch – the ability to pitch a note exactly. This is certainly not a pre-requisite for musical ability and indeed many successful musicians do not have perfect pitch. It is an innate skill which nevertheless can be extremely useful for aspiring musicians. Similarly, some people seem to be born with a heightened sense of rhythm: they are able to sustain a complicated rhythmic pattern where others struggle to clap on the offbeat. And in the same way, one child is gifted with a strong, tuneful voice, where another can't find the right note to sing. In many cases these talents may go undiscovered if the opportunities for music making are limited during a child's upbringing.

It is clear however, that many of these skills can be acquired through nurture. Through the regular and repetitive tuning of guitars and other instruments over the years for example, I have acquired memory pitch. A child with a weak, slightly out of tune singing voice can be coached to strengthen tone and pitch and produce creditable results.

So how does a child become a musician? As with many skills and talents, the answer probably lies somewhere in a complex balance of nature and nurture, with the latter involving the careful provision of example, opportunity, advice, and guidance which itself strikes a balance between technical instruction, imitation and the encouragement of creativity. Furthermore, the encouragement of musical skills in our children can lead to enhanced development in other areas.

'By bringing out and exercising musical ability in children, you nurture the development of their intelligence.'[9]

'Recent reports show that piano playing increases the spatial ability of children. Now it seems that singing uses the same mental skills: the simple act of singing changes the way the brain "thinks" about music.'[10]

Which came first – the music or the music?

There are several different approaches to learning musical skills. Some people learn to play music by subscribing to the 'you hum it, I'll play it' school where imitation or 'playing by ear' is the main method; others learn by reading the 'dots'. There are obvious parallels with language here: the comparisons with listening to and telling stories as opposed to writing them down and reading. In both music and spoken/written language, we must beware that the medium for transmission does not transcend the content.

'Music' means different things to different people. For some, the study of music is the creation and interpretation of the written form – in its extreme form, music can become an academic exercise. There are very many excellent musicians who play purely from written music; take this away and they can play very little. At the other end of the spectrum are the musicians who have a natural feel for the music they play and often compose and improvise without any written music at all. Many jazz and folk musicians would fall into this category. However, the majority of musicians probably fall somewhere between the extremes of the spectrum using a combination of skills, both written and aural to interpret their music.

Making music with children

Music is a very acceptable and integral part of early years development both at home and elsewhere. The proliferation of Family Music Clubs particularly bears witness to this. These provide sessions where parents or carers and children can enjoy musical activities together. However useful these are, there is usually only the potential for part of the family to participate, and there is still much opportunity for more inclusive music making in the home.

The recently published guidance document on teaching phonic skills, 'Letters & Sounds', places great emphasis on the development of sound discrimination skills including musical elements as a precursor to literacy. In its 'Phase 1' section it encourages: listening to and playing simple percussion instruments; making up new songs to familiar tunes; action songs – including clapping; stamping to a beat; different ways of moving and body percussion. It advocates learning through much imitation and emulation.[11]

All these can be used as a starting point for making music together in the home with young children and have the added bonus of developing useful skills in your child. For example, rhythm games can help to develop auditory memory. The High Scope project identified the ability to keep a steady beat – or 'beat competency' as one of the best predictors of later academic success.[12]

Start with clapping hands and playing pat-a-cake, and when your child is old enough, walk, march, jump, hop and skip together to music. Use any style of music – as long as it's something you both enjoy. Sing along … and sing in the bath! Lullabies, songs involving actions, movement, bouncing up and down, etc., all add to the experience. You can use songs that were sung to you when you were young, or popular songs from any period – traditional nursery rhymes and songs have survived over the years for good reason – they're easy to sing and memorable. This is where true folk music occurs (interpreting the term as meaning traditional music transmitted orally). Make up your own songs: use simple words and phases and sing them to an easy tune – use someone else's if you're not that confident. Remember, the lyrics don't have to be high-class poetry! Non-rhymes can sometimes seem very funny indeed to young children! Always include lots of clapping along, and other physical actions. If you feel that your musical abilities are very limited, use the wealth of pre-recorded CDs aimed at early years music making to form a basis for your home activities. As they get older, encourage them to interact more with you using 'follow my leader' styles of songs. And listen to music with your children, whether passively or actively: introduce them to as many different musical styles as possible. Remember music can soothe as well as excite!

Introduce percussion instruments at an early age. As a child's motor skills increase they will enjoy shaking, hitting and scraping a variety of instruments – many of which can easily be home-made. Try encouraging them to make regular patterns of sound and then join in adding new rhythms – form your own family percussion group!

By the time children reach school age, they are able to assimilate vast amounts of musical information. Many 5 year olds can sing a whole pop song word and note perfect, whereas their parents probably struggle to remember the chorus! From this stage onwards, look for signs that your child might want to learn to play an instrument. Don't force the issue, but provide the opportunities. There is no optimum age for this: different children will be ready at different times. A child who starts an instrument at the age of 7 may make slower progress than a child who starts at 9 and is therefore more capable. They will quite probably reach the same point of competency at the same time. Conversely however there are some children who when given an instrument at an early age never look back. Be ready when your child shows interest to encourage and provide opportunities – and if you don't play anything yourself, take up the challenge and learn too – there is no age limit!

What instrument should my child play?

While there are numerous books on selecting the right instrument for your child perhaps the easiest answer is – the one they really want to play! It may be the same instrument as a parent or sibling or a friend – and the advantage here would be that advice on how to play (and maybe an instrument) is readily available. But arguably it's better for them to have their own instrument, which will help to be part of their identity. This also allows for complementary playing at home.

Encourage your child to see role models – both on TV and live. Many of us, as both children and adults have experienced a 'That's what I want to do' or 'I could do that' moment, and watching accomplished role models provides aspiration and inspiration.

Discuss the adaptability of different instruments, and the styles of music that are played by that instrument. For example an instrument such as an oboe will mostly be played in orchestras whereas a violin can be an orchestral instrument but is also widely used in folk and country music and also occasionally in popular music. Trumpets likewise can crossover from pop to jazz to orchestral music.

There may also be physical constraints when a small child starts to learn an instrument, such as size of hands. For example, not everyone is physically big enough to play the largest instrument in the saxophone family, the baritone saxophone, but there are others to choose from if the dream is to play this instrument: a good place to start is with the much smaller alto sax. For many instruments, small-sized versions are readily available. Violins come in quarter, half and three-quarter sizes before you need to play a full size instrument. Nowadays there are also small clarinets, trumpets and trombones available to start on as well as child-friendly versions of instruments such as 'curved-head' flutes. Size should not be a deterrent!

There is also a raft of instruments more specifically used in popular music such as guitars, bass guitars and drums. While the popularity of various instruments can be subject to fashion related to the pop-music of the day, the guitar has been a widely used instrument since the mid-twentieth century and the recent indie-rock and acoustic club movements bear witness to its resurgence in the early twenty-first century.

The advantages of playing the guitar in an age which values individualism and creativity are many. The guitar provides rhythm and harmony through strumming chords, over which melodies can be created, with or without lyrics. An acoustic guitar is also easy for someone to sing over un-amplified – in many different moods and styles. The versatility of the guitar is also extended by the electric guitar, which can be a most effective lead instrument.

It may be necessary to take into account the other instruments being played at home (most homes would struggle to accommodate two drum kits!): ideally a complementary selection of instruments will encourage a more rounded family music-making experience, but don't worry if two of your children both want to play the trumpet – you have a ready made brass section! One family I knew all played stringed instruments but as this ranged from violin to viola and cello, they were able to play string quartets together. By chance (and it really was chance, as we let each child choose their own instruments) we have all the elements of a rock/pop/jazz band within my own family.

Whatever your child chooses to play, start right from the beginning with them, encouraging them and providing opportunities for them to play within the family as well as elsewhere.

Music: A shared experience

'Children who take part in music develop higher levels of social cohesion and understanding of themselves and others, and the emotional aspect of musical activities seems to be beneficial for developing social skills like empathy'.[13]

However musical skills are acquired, sooner or later in our lives we meet with shared musical or rhythmic experiences. It is clear that group music making helps us to learn how to work together, but it goes further than that. It also has the power to unite us socially and emotionally.

Singing together in a choir, or playing in a band or orchestra, gives us a sense of belonging and camaraderie, of working together for a common cause, the sum of whose parts seems to be greater than the individual contributions. And again, where specific words are incorporated the result can be an even greater feeling of identity, mutual purpose and worth. Traditionally, national anthems and school songs were sung to motivate, unite and encourage loyalty. In the workplace company songs have sometimes been used for the same purpose. And of course the liturgy of many religious services has been greatly enhanced by music over the years. The corporate nature of these experiences has been undermined in recent years by the pursuit of individualism, and yet the singing of a national anthem at a major sporting event still has the power to move, inspiring unity and loyalty.

This feeling of togetherness needs to be valued at all levels of music making; from the chants of sports crowds and protesters to the sophisticated playing of an orchestra. Many schools still recite multiplication tables to promote fluency of thought and recollection and there are many historical examples of call and response (both spoken and sung) which enhance many group situations, whether it be a call to spiritual worship in a church or a motivator for physical action such as a sea shanty or a Negro spiritual.

Musical aspiration and attitudes

As we have seen, music is universal, and can be enjoyed at all levels. There are however aspects of music that present challenges to our social, emotional and intellectual wellbeing, many of them linked to attitude and aspiration. Attitudes towards music can be as diverse as attitudes towards family life.

For some, music is an ambient part of their lifestyle: others see music as a diversion or a distraction from everyday life. For many it is a hobby to be enjoyed. Others see music as a driving force in their lives. Perhaps they want to make a career in music or it becomes their way of gaining respect from their peers. (And this can apply as much to the middle-aged as it does to the teenage bands!) Yet again, others see music purely as a focus for academic study. (Attending a recent Open Day at the music department of a leading English university, one of my daughters was told: 'If you come to this college you must understand that you're not here to enjoy music, you're not here to play music, you're not here to listen to music, you're here to *study* music.')

At whatever level we approach music, we all expect to achieve some success. As in many other aspects of life, 'success' is directly linked to our levels of expectation, ambition and satisfaction, and our own perception of what constitutes 'success'. Do we have a level at which we are quite happy to stay, or do we have an insatiable drive to search, perhaps in vain, for the ultimate goal and better ourselves to a point which may never be reached?

I used to play in a band with adults who represented both ends of this particular spectrum. One band member was more than happy to tap along to folk tunes on a simple percussion instrument: he gained huge personal satisfaction from being part of the band, knowing that his contribution was a valuable part of the overall sound, and yet he never desired to try anything more complicated than a simple rhythm. Alongside him was a young instrumentalist who was continually striving to be better: playing ever more complicated and technically difficult music and starting to compose tunes – he has now achieved national and international recognition for his playing. For these two musicians, the expectations were vastly different, but the level of enjoyment and satisfaction was the same.

Sometimes however, aspiration can lead to perspiration and ultimately frustration! We sweat away at something to achieve a goal, only to find that everyone else is already there! There are many who have been discouraged from playing music or even stopped playing, because they feel that they'll never be as good as the next person. And there are those who would question the musical credentials of others who have not reached the musical standards that they have. Sometimes parents encourage their children to take up an instrument because they regret giving up too soon themselves.

Music inevitably has its competitive element. For example, the learning process can often be punctuated by graded exams which are essential motivators and indicators of standard for some, but can inevitably lead to comparisons. And many musicians often spend their time assessing fellow performers – are they as good as me? As Trish comments in the opening chapter, we live in a world of experts! Whatever we do, there always seems to be someone there telling us we could have done it better, or that the way we are doing something is wrong. And the musical world is full of them! Performing in public can mean running the gauntlet of close scrutiny, comparison and judgement.

But with such a diverse and subjective an area as music, it is as well to remember that we all have different opinions and tastes. Popular music in particular is so prone to fashion and fad; today's must-have musical style is tomorrow's uncool music of yesterday. What constitutes good music can be radically different for different people.

Within all this the musician has to find his or her own level of aspiration. Unfortunately our modern culture has a tendency to offer many false aspirations in the world of music.

Perhaps one of the motivations for young people to make music is the lure of fame and fortune. While this has always been a potential motivator for some, the recent popularity of TV shows such as *Pop Idol* and *The X Factor* bear witness to the burgeoning numbers of people who see music as a short cut to a lavish lifestyle. The reality is that we have made an entertainment out of watching people's musical (and other) aspirations collapse around them. As Caitlin Moran in a sardonic review of the fourth series of *The X Factor* for *The Times* said: 'As the *X Factor* cruises into its fourth schedule-dominating season … it's clear that … around 84 per cent of the population of Great Britain is a truly eccentric, truly untalented, wannabe pop star'.[14]

Musical aspiration has also been extended by the development of digital technology, which has revolutionized the way in which popular music is produced and has created a wealth of opportunities at all levels. It is now no longer necessary for a band to record a piece of music together. In many cases it is commonplace for the basic instrumental tracks of a song to be recorded and then emailed (sometimes half way across the world!) for the vocalist to add their part. Live recordings of instruments and vocals can be edited to alter pitch, rhythm and tone. If you don't like the way you've sung one chorus of a song, you can cut and paste in a better one! We can embrace the benefits of modern technology but as in many other areas of our lives, the increase in capability through the digital revolution has led to an increase in expectation of standard. We expect all music now to be perfect, because we are hearing near perfect recordings on CDs and radio. Unfortunately, as a consequence of this, live performance is often a disappointment.

To get our aspirations into perspective, we need to have the right attitudes. Our children are very much a part of the high expectation generation and the need for instant gratification has pervaded many areas of their lives, including music. We need to foster a realistic approach to music making: aspirations should be high but realistic, tolerance of others' musical ability should be encouraged, and while competition can be a useful motivator it should not be pursued for its own sake. Above all, making music should be enjoyable and fun, and should provide our children with skills which will enhance their lives at whatever level they choose to use them. And an excellent way of fostering all of the above is to make music an integral part of family life at all ages and stages.

> Through experiencing music, our children will learn about balance, about making choices and decisions, and about finding their own levels of satisfaction.

Musicality in the family

The family is an excellent context for the shared experience of music. While there may be severe time restraints within our busy family lives – not least the lure of the screen (TV or computer) – time invested in family music making at whatever age, will be time well spent. Historically there have been many methods of music teaching which have placed an emphasis on the value of home learning and the involvement of parents. One of the best known of these is the Suzuki method: Suzuki taught that sounds should precede signs in the learning process and music technique and sensitivity can be learnt through imitation and emulation – the family should all participate in instrumental study.[15]

Whose responsibility is it to make music with a child?

This is perhaps the same question as whose responsibility is it to teach a child to tell stories, read, write or draw pictures?

While many of these skills are begun at home (although decreasingly so, as many foundation stage teachers will testify), once a child has begun school there is an increasing tendency for the parents to draw back. This is often because parents see it as the role of the school to teach these skills and they are frightened to persist with their own tuition in these areas for fear of confusing their child, or giving a mixed message. So to what extent should we develop talents with our children, read and write with our children, draw with our children, make music with our children, and to what extent do we leave it to the skilled 'experts'?

Having been involved in primary school education for over 25 years, I am a firm believer in the necessity for a partnership between home and school, with a strong dialogue between the two, to maximize a child's learning experience. Once again, the answer lies in balance. We can start in the home with encouragement and the establishment of positive attitudes through play, and the example of our own enjoyment. While we may not necessarily have the skills, we should certainly have the enthusiasm and interest. And depending on our own abilities we can contribute and learn alongside our children.

And this does not just mean the child learning from parents, but mutual whole-family learning, between peers and across generations.

This all applies too to music making. We can start in the home, encouraging and sharing musical experiences with our children and then work towards a balance of shared responsibility with the educators. The problems can often arise when the balance is tilted too far in one direction. On the one hand, music making should not be exclusively a family activity. In order for us all to be well-rounded, balanced and useful members of society we need to interact with society and joining music groups within and outside school can provide social networks and interaction in the same way as other activities such as sport. Children should be encouraged to take advantage of as many music-making opportunities as they wish to. Conversely however, sometimes as children move into the school music system they do so at the expense of family music. While it is well recognized that sharing music with your pre-school child is expected of all 'good' parents, too often on entering school, a child's group music-making experience is taken over by a formal, school setting. A shared family musical experience need not end when children are old enough to join school groups.

The biggest bar to this is the way in which once a child progresses through the school music system, often ending up in an external schools music service, the activity becomes age related and most musical interaction takes place in peer groups. By this stage, in many families, parents have usually been relegated to fund raising, supporting concerts and administrative tasks and have lost the practical family-based musical working together that characterizes pre-school development. Furthermore, and disappointingly, some teachers positively discourage parents from assisting in their child's musical development. The wealth of potential skill and wisdom which cross-generational music making can exploit often lies dormant. There is in fact no reason why parents can't contribute to and maintain their children's musical activities from within the family through practical music making together regardless of age or individual standards of competence. As always, the optimum is a balance between parents, children and professional educators with encouragement and skills shared at all levels and between all ages.

Pass it on

In an age of distance learning, university for all, targets and qualifications, we seem to have lost sight of one of the most effective ways of learning: the time-honoured system of apprenticeship – passing skills on through example, in particular from 'older and wiser' generations. From my own experience of organizing community arts activities based around schools I can vouch for the huge benefits of inter-generational collaboration.

However, in this day and age, cross-generational music making is not very common and tends to be very genre dependent. Nevertheless it does still occur in specific areas. For example in the UK the brass band movement is noted for its family involvement, and in both the UK and the US, traditional folk music tends to include a mix of ages, as well as an accepted element of family music making (the Carter family dynasty in America being one of the best-known examples). Furthermore in the days before radio and recorded music, entertainment often came in the form of a village band where old and young combined to produce music for communal events.

Clearly in many of these cases, the expectation is that the older generation has musical skills that they can pass on, and if this is the case – why not? Why not involve parents, grandparents and other extended family members in your child's music making – and where families are fragmented, involve those who have become surrogate family members whether blood relations or not. And yet, playing in a band that spans two generations, I've lost count of the times that someone has said to me 'You know, I play an instrument, and my children play – but we've never played together – ever.' I always think – and sometimes say – 'Why not????'

Making music together as a family unit can have mutual benefits. Not only do the younger generation learn musical, collaborative and social skills from their elders, but the older generation can be inspired by the enthusiasm and vitality of younger members. So if you have musical skills yourself, however rudimentary, share them with your children and rope in everyone else!

Will you turn that noise down? – Closing the generation gap

As recently as ten years ago, there was still a perceived generation gap with regard to musical tastes, and some parenting books from that period portray preference for a particular style of music as a potential generational battleground. For example, in his guide for teenagers *Bringing up your Parents*, John Farman writes 'Every generation thinks their parents' music is old-fashioned – and parents think their children's taste is too modern. Can you imagine your dad bursting into your room and asking if you could turn the volume up a bit because he really likes it ... ? I think not.'[16]

While this may still be the case in some families, I believe that over the past few years this viewpoint has become increasingly less true.

The growth of popular music in the second half of the twentieth century was seen primarily as something for the 'young people': on the whole, older people neither played nor had any interest in the popular music scene. This, however, is changing, with old and young generations bonding together, both in creating new music together and referencing the music of past generations.

The last few years have seen little radical innovation in terms of musical style. Many of the 'popular' bands of the early twenty-first century are unashamedly transparent in their admiration for, and readily accept the influence of, bands which were popular 30 or more years ago (presumably when they were growing up at home, and as pre-teens, listening to their parents' record collections). Numerous bands such as The Who, The Beatles, Def Leppard and Queen are still in vogue, despite being formed up to 40 years ago. Pop music is no longer always dividing families: it's now a case of 'Have you taken my record again?' rather than 'Turn that racket off!' From a personal viewpoint – I don't necessarily like *all* the music my children listen to, and vice versa. But I don't regard this as a generational difference, more a question of personal preference – this is our prerogative as individuals. Music will always have its divisions, whether they be between amateur and professional, popular and classical, down to differences within genres, such as the differences between 'Emos' and 'Goths', both of which are bracketed under the 'alternative rock' sector of the commercial music market. Age, however, particularly in the rock genre of popular music, is increasingly becoming less of a divisive issue. Instead of tearing the teenagers and the adults apart, music is becoming the social pacifier and common ground that can bring generations closer together.

Moreover, the huge increase in accessibility to music has helped to narrow the generational divide. Recently, the Arts Council England stated that: 'more people than ever – young people, adults, professionals, amateurs – are playing, singing, creating their own music'.[17] Older generations are becoming increasingly involved in practical music making, with 44 per cent of the adult population claiming to play a musical instrument, and with many households having more disposable income to spend on ever-cheaper musical instruments and home-recording equipment. And the increasing use of the internet by all ages has encouraged an explosion of musical interaction ranging from downloading music to networking with other musicians. Social networking sites such as MySpace allow many unsigned bands to promote their music across the world, and when you look at the profiles of these bands, a considerable number have older-age profiles. Quite simply, with the anonymity of the internet, age is no longer an issue: for today's popular music lovers, it's more about the music than how old the people are that are making it.

Aspects of 'Cool'

To a greater or lesser extent we all worry about what others will think about us, and as children develop their independence, *their* idea of what is 'cool' (and perhaps more importantly to them, that of their peers) may change and develop under the fierce glare of the media and the marketing industries. What is and what isn't socially acceptable assumes huge importance. We cling to the familiar for security but search for the new in an attempt to validate our own value and values. For many young people, music is a way of establishing their own unique identity. Look at the MySpace pages of emerging young bands where the band is asked to define their musical genre, and the answer to the phrase 'Our band sounds like ...' is often '... nothing else'! Everyone is trying to establish their individuality, and wanting to be 'different'.

And there is a certainly a case for encouraging teenagers who, in forming a band, are flexing the wings of their independence, in a situation where, unlike school or home, there isn't an authority figure there to tell them what they must do. Unfortunately, many parents approach their offspring's teenage band with resigned tolerance. How often I have heard a parent say of their child 'Oh yes, he's/she's in a band – they make an unspeakable noise in the spare room.' And yet, talking further, you find that the same parent is in reality proud of their child's involvement. A child learning to play the violin can also produce unspeakable noises but it is all part of the learning process of expressing different forms of musicality. A family unit should be able to absorb all the pressures and trials of music making (whatever the genre) in a non-judgemental way. We shouldn't need to worry about being cool within our own homes.

Music can also be a channel for making a statement about other issues. For example, the 'punk' movement of the late 1970s, and early 1980s was often associated with extreme right-wing groups. Similarly, rap and hip-hop is very much seen as the music of the urban culture. Music can polarise: race, cultures, age groups, religions, political standpoints have all 'claimed' musical styles and used them as identifying labels. So by choosing to follow a particular band you are often saying something about yourself and who you are – and showing your peers that you are 'cool'.

So is playing music as a family a 'cool' activity?

Playing together: Family banned?

The general perception of family bands is not positive. In 2003 an article in *Sound on Sound* magazine which featured our family's home-recording studio began:

> '… the entertainment was provided by a family band comprising parents and their three daughters. Normally this type of line-up, especially when all three girls are still at school, is a recipe for hopelessly cheesy music and sympathy based applause …'[18].

While the article continued in a very complimentary way, the preconceptions are clear to see.

And these preconceptions have been repeated to us many times as we have played as a band. We have often seen a certain apprehension in the faces of the audience before we start playing, that because the band is a family, somehow this is going to be something rather embarrassing and poor quality! When audiences watch adults play they're looking for a 'wow factor' rather than the 'ahh factor' they will enjoy from a child's performance. However once we start playing and the barriers are broken down, the audience starts to enjoy the music for what it is and when we finish, it has suddenly become completely acceptable to be cross-generational. Then the positives start to reveal themselves with comments such as: 'Isn't it great that you all play together', 'Wish we'd done more music making as a family when the kids were little', 'Must be because you're sisters that the voices blend so well'. And the compliments come from peers of both generations.

The last comment really shows one of the pluses of making music as a family. Because your children have common genes, the chances are quite high that they will relate well musically and complement each other's skills. That's not to say that every member will have the same level of skill or aptitude, but it is possible to include everyone in some capacity or other.

By playing as a family you are in fact following a well-trodden path. Before the advent of radio and television, music was often an integral part of family life – as an important part of family entertainment. The inclusion of a class for family music making in many local music festivals is a relic from the past which unfortunately, in many cases, fails to attract many entries these days. Family music making can be purely within the home and for our own pleasure. The dynamics change somewhat when the music is taken out of the home and into public performance. Naturally, this has to be with the agreement of all participants and needn't necessarily involve a full-blown 'band' situation. Playing together as a family within a larger group (as in the brass band culture for example) can be equally rewarding. Any public performance involves new challenges for a group, many of which can strengthen character.

Living out our fantasies through our children – and other thorny issues!

It is a common parental feeling to wish for our children the things that we didn't have ourselves, be it possessions or skills, academic or financial success. And it is an easy step for parents to transfer their desires and aspirations to their children.

One only has to attend (or worse still referee!) a junior school football match to feel the pressure, aggression and unconcealed ambition of the parents on the touchline. The same can be very true of music. There is a fine balance to maintain here. Do our children participate in activities because they want to – or because we want them to? Conversely, do we sometimes not pass things on because we feel we might be pushing them into something they don't want? Most children have an inbuilt desire to want to please their parents – they want them to be proud of them. As they grow older the need to be encouraged and appreciated reveals itself in different ways – sometimes it is not obvious at all, but it is still there. As parents we have the tricky task of finding that middle way between encouraging a child without suffocating them, steering them without dictating to them and making sure that they are not engaging in something purely because they think it will please us. And at the same time we have to respect their sensitivities. Of course we are proud when our children achieve – but our view of their talents is perhaps not the most objective, and parents are sometimes guilty of over-extolling the merits of their offspring to the acute embarrassment of the child. We can all be guilty of pushing our child into something to obtain some reflected glory. As music is a performance art, there is always going to be ample scope for all of the above!

The key to dealing with these issues is not to see our children as extensions of ourselves, but as separate individuals. We also need to keep the lines of communication open. As both a teacher and parent – and as adults in society, I feel that we have a strong responsibility to provide channels of opportunity. But the ultimate decision as to whether or not those opportunities are pursued has to rest with the child.

What's the cost?

Another barrier to participating in music can be the cost of instruments and lessons; while for some it is a question of financial priorities, for others this cost is prohibitive. Until fairly recently in the UK, most subsidized music was channelled through schools or organized social projects. However there has recently been a move towards schemes for loan/subsidized purchase available to private individuals by bodies such as Arts Council England – and this is to be welcomed.

Starting a family band

Family music making sessions should be:

- **Inclusive** – everybody who wants to should be able to join in – ideally, encourage the whole family to participate.

- **Unforced** – while you need loyalty and commitment in order for it to be a valuable experience, it has to be voluntary.

- **Not a performance** – an 'audience' of non-participants can make you feel self-conscious, and as though you're performing, rather than just creating music together.

- **Often spontaneous**.

- **Producing music to a standard that satisfies you** – it doesn't have to be professional standard to be enjoyable!

- **An ego-free zone!!** – don't make it a competition: be proud of each other's achievements. Learning alongside your child can produce an interesting shift in relationships when they become more capable than you! My children outstripped my musical abilities many years ago, but this has not stopped us playing together. And we still have much to learn from each other!

And last but not least ...

FUN!

Above all, a family band is about inclusion: working out strategies for the least able musicians (whether because of age or ability) to take a part. With young children, the key is to challenge but to allow each player to play within their own capabilities.

These roles may change – as the children get older and more accomplished, they will quite probably take the lead – and while some parents may find this quite difficult to accept others are more than happy to take a backseat role in the family band. (Isn't this a reflection of family life itself?)

A family band could consist of the elements:

- Percussion
- Bass/Harmony (Chords)
- Melody.

A good way to introduce young children into the family band is to let them play the chords. At the simplest level (from the age of 4 or 5 upwards) this can involve playing an automatic keyboard, with coloured stickers on the appropriate keys. Repetitive chord progressions are simple to play. With only three different chords (the 'three chord trick' – based on the first, fourth and fifth notes of a major scale) you can play many popular songs. The skills they will learn from this simple inclusion will include keeping in time with everyone else and hearing when it's time to change chord. This can then lead on to playing the full chords themselves either on the keyboard, or perhaps on a different instrument such as the guitar.

Playing together – 'The one-note boogie' and other musical enablers

Have you heard about the little girl who wanted to play?

She practised on the saxophone every day.

But she'd only had one lesson, it's true,

And playing one note was all she could do.

She played the one-note boogie,

She played the one-note boogie,

She played the one-note boogie,

Playing on the saxophone every day.

As a 6 year old, one of my daughter's favourite pieces on her newly acquired saxophone was the 'One-note boogie'! (see above), a home-made song, where she played the one note she could play, every other bar. It sounded great – and she was part of the band. Writing that one note on manuscript paper began her musical literacy. (It soon turned into the two-note boogie, and now she plays – and writes – saxophone concertos!)

As a teacher I was also very keen to get the children in my school playing together and spent many an hour writing individual parts for them, even though some of them could only play three or four notes. But if those three or four notes are played in the right place, you're doing your job as part of the band – and when you can play more notes, a more complex part can be found. These arrangements often contained a lot of chord playing (long notes) underneath a tune played by the more able players. (Note for musical teachers/ parents – the key of F major is good for beginners – notes in the three main chords can be played on open strings on violins, and it is also an easy key for the B♭ instruments such as clarinets and trumpets!) Nowadays many simple arrangements for school bands are available to purchase and these can also easily be adapted and used for family music making.

Waxing lyrical

The style of music you play will depend on your own taste or cultural background. You can either choose to play existing tunes or songs – from one generation or another – or make up your own!

We have the technology

Accessibility to home-recording equipment has added a further dimension to family music making. Relatively cheap, but high-quality equipment often linked to computer sequencing software, has opened the way for opportunities for families to create reasonable quality tracks, either using sequencers or live instruments. Home recordings can be both a source of pride, and a great record of achievement. MySpace and other similar internet sites have opened up the possibilities of sharing your music with others should you so wish – recordings of your family music can go global!

'I'd like to teach the world to sing in perfect harmony'

Musical elements as an analogy for family life

Many parallels can be drawn between playing in a band, and being a family. This final section explores some of the elements needed in a musical band, and thereby raises issues about what makes a successful family.

Meet the band ...

A band comprises a group of people working together to achieve a shared objective. The number of people and the personnel can vary, but complementary skills and roles co-ordinated through teamwork and co-operation, with much communication and listening to each other, should enable successful outcomes.

The style of music produced may vary from band to band and with it, the exact line-up of instruments, but as a band plays, the essential ingredients of rhythm, harmony and melody blend together to form a distinctive and unique sound. When all the elements are in place, we need to check constantly that they are in tune with each other and that the balance of the band is right so that the overall result – whatever the chosen genre – is a pleasing one.

So it is with a family; the blend of individual personalities will determine the nature of family life. And where there is an awareness of each other's roles and needs, supported by sympathetic listening and mutual respect, the outcome will be pleasing.

For our line-up I have chosen a combination of instruments familiar in many genres of popular western music:

Rhythm is usually established by the drums.

Harmony is played through sustained chords on an instrument, underpinned by a bass instrument (often a bass guitar or double bass). These chords are played in rhythm – closely with the drums.

The **melody** plays itself out supported by and following the structure of the rhythm and harmony.

These basic elements can be paralleled in family life.

The band		The family
Rhythm	Drums	Routines, patterns
Harmony	Bass	Values, standards, beliefs
	Guitar / Keyboards	Environment and diet, activities, ambience, surroundings
Melody	Lead instruments (or vocals)	Taking the lead, life experiences

Percussive parenting – you can't beat it! Rhythm and routine in daily life

'All child development experts point to the significance of regularity and routine in children's lives.'[19]

A standard drum kit (although there are many variations on the basic configuration) consists of drums and cymbals played together by both hands and feet in a co-ordinated way.

The **bass drum** sets the pace – it plays the strong first beat, often at a walking pace. But it needs to be constant. Think of it being the sound of your right foot as you walk. And the **snare drum** supports the bass drum – often they play together – a bit like the left and right foot in a steady walking pace.

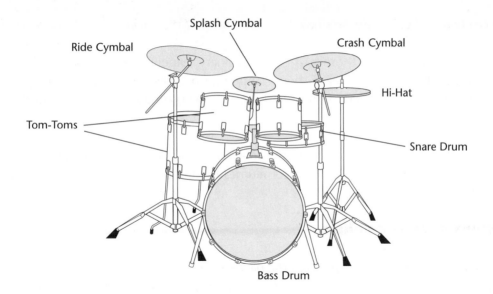

Splash Cymbal

Ride Cymbal

Crash Cymbal

Hi-Hat

Tom-Toms

Snare Drum

Bass Drum

These regular beats form the basic structure of our lifestyle so that we know what to expect. Things like mealtimes, bedtimes, and school routines provide a framework for our daily lives.

Of course a simple rhythm can become boring and repetitive so you can play different patterns on the bass drum and snare to elaborate the basic beats.

If we stuck with the same routine day after day, we would soon become bored and life would seem very mundane. So it is good to introduce some elaboration to the basic patterns. Weekends are a chance to change the routine and evening activities during the week can add more variety to the basic structure.

*The **Hi-Hat** consists of two cymbals placed on top of each other. These are often played to a steady rhythm but they add a more percussive element. The other cymbals in a drum kit add a bright sound. They are not played all the time but are used to give highlights of colour and a push to the rhythm.*

Every now and again we need to do something dramatic – make a different noise, break out of the normal routines, do something special to bring a highlight to our lives.

***Tom-Toms** – Take a break! – occasionally something different happens to the rhythm; there is a pause in the music and it is filled by a break on the **Tom-Toms**. Sometimes they can even go solo!*

To keep things interesting, we need breaks from the routine, perhaps involving other things: holidays, trips to see relatives – maybe for a while, a new routine in a different place.

Crash cymbals and splash cymbals have a special sound of their own.

Occasionally in life we have those 'out-of-the-ordinary' experiences. Sometimes they just happen to us, other times we make them happen for ourselves. But whatever they may be, they provide the inspiration that often keeps us going through the more mundane times.

As we co-ordinate all these elements in our family routines, we produce a unique and distinctive shape to our lives; although sometimes the tempo might increase – making it seem a bit more difficult to keep up!

Harmony – Bass-ic values

The bass guitar, or double bass, provides the pitched rhythm which works in time with the drums, playing the main beats of the bar. It is the driving force that gives depth to the sound, underpinning all the other harmony instruments.

We need to add this element of underpinning to the rhythm and routine of family life. Values, beliefs and morals provide a starting point on which to build for other activities. Whether we use religious or secular frameworks, we must have some code of behaviour to teach our children. This code or set of values must at the very least teach a sense of right and wrong and a sense of respect for others. We teach this to our children through words, actions and example and it underpins and forms the bass line for all our activities. I often wonder whether modern society has lost the bass line.

Harmony – Chords and discords

Harmony is the combination of simultaneously sounded musical notes. Harmony instruments can include guitars and keyboards, both of which have the facility to play more than one note together. When several notes are played together, they form chords. With the right combination of notes they provide very pleasing sounds, but put a note in that doesn't gel with the others and you get discords.

Building on our morals and values are the chords of family life: the ambience of our children's environment. This includes a combination of factors relating to home life: the surroundings in which we live, the activities we indulge in and even the type of food we eat. These all need to blend together in a harmonious way or the result will be discord! Much has been written recently about the lack of exercise, poor diet and excesses of television and computers in the lives of our children today and it is up to parents to get the balance right within their own home. But it is more than this: it is about striking the right chords in terms of environment. Taking care to ensure that potential hazards in the home are dealt with appropriately for the age of your children; allowing spaces where it's safe to play – and OK to make a mess! Providing appropriate equipment in the home (from toys and computers to furniture, clothes, and consumables such as paper) and ensuring a balance between human and electronic interaction will all help to add the right notes to the chord. This extends further as our children move into friendship groups and school environments. All these factors blended together will also dictate their moods, feelings and attitudes in the same way that musical chords can change moods according to their composition.

Melody – Taking the tune

Rhythm and harmony provide a good basis for a band sound but on their own are incomplete. What is needed is some type of melody to provide a tune. This can be played on a variety of instruments or, as in many cases, sung. The melody takes the lead and provides the most memorable part of any musical item. And the other members of the band have to follow the lead of the vocalist or instrumentalist taking the tune, although occasionally the keyboard or the guitar for example may take over the tune for a while. However, if the melody is poorly performed (out of time or out of tune for example), it affects the whole performance of the band. Likewise, if the rhythm section dominates the band sound it can mar the balance of the music.

So who comes first in your family? As with any group activity, there needs to be someone who provides a lead. The obvious answer for a family situation is the parents, and it is only right that as older (and hopefully wiser!) adults, they should take this role. Certainly in the early years of a child's life, the parents will play the tune, making decisions, taking the responsibility for the overall 'sound' of family life in both practical and emotional ways. But as children grow older, they can start to take on some of these responsibilities. Helping out with jobs in the home, taking responsibility for a pet, looking after younger siblings: all these activities help children to develop their own leadership roles in a safe, supportive environment.

Problems can arise, however, when the balance is upset. Perhaps one member of the family is becoming too strident, not allowing other members to play their parts properly. Sometimes, one child can be more extrovert and attention seeking than their sibling and it is all too easy for time poor, stressed parents to give in to one at the expense of the other. Occasionally, the balance is all wrong and it is the inexperienced children who are calling the tune, holding their parents to ransom, without deliberately meaning to. The parent who gives in to their screaming child rather than let it cause a scene is storing up potential leadership battles for the future. Within any family, and indeed any band, there needs to be discipline. You cannot lead without it. The parameters of performance need to be set and adhered to. It is easy to write this, but of course with families, as with bands, it isn't always easy to implement – we are only human after all (and often tired, stressed, anxious humans to boot!), but that shouldn't stop us from trying. It's all too easy to give in and give up. The most successful bands have had their fair share of angst along the way, but have had to persist to make the whole work. So too with the family: aspire to make the best melody you can.

Strike up the band . . .

When forming a band there are various other aspects to take into account and many of these also have useful parallels with family life.

Following the dots

'Following the dots' is musician-speak for reading from music ('dots' being the musical notes). Most musicians at whatever level, need written music to enable them to play, whether it's simple recorder music or a Beethoven sonata. Sometimes they learn the pieces by heart and perform from memory, but having a piece written down means that it is always played the same. There are, however, other musicians who can't read a note of music but still instinctively understand how to put a piece of music together. To have both sets of skills allows for more adaptability in music making.

When it comes to parenting there is always plenty of advice to be had. Over the years, hundreds of books have been published telling parents how to look after their children, usually following the accepted wisdom of the era in which they were written. Some parenting manuals contain rigid advice about how to deal with your child, others advocate an unstructured approach. So do we follow the score – or make it up as we go along?

Many of these volumes (old and new) contain useful advice and most parents will have at the very least a book about childhood ailments. We need something written down to give us the courage and confidence to take on some of the more daunting tasks of parenthood. But just as everyone has at least some small musical ability within them, so it is with parenting. We have times when we don't need to read from the music because we have an intuition for what is needed for our child. Some styles of music are more prescriptive than others – and we choose what types of music to play. But don't forget to be a natural musician.

You hum it, I'll play it

While music has a very detailed and intricate system of transcription, it is ultimately a human activity, and it is notoriously complicated to write or to create technologically music that has the human 'give' that often defines the most emotionally satisfying pieces we listen to. Written forms can transmit content; the contextual qualities of that content – the tone, pitch and expression are more difficult to record. But these things can be learnt through imitation. It is common in the jazz world to ask a player who their influences are – jazz musicians often model their style on other well-known players. Some learn to improvise by studying and imitating the solos of the 'greats'.

We all learn from each other. Many communication skills, including those of linguistics and music, rely on imitation. In the same way our children will learn life skills from the role models around them and of course that usually means the parents. Whatever the patterns, routines, values and environment that we provide for our children, the whole will be infused with our own tone, expression and personalized style.

As parents, we need to think carefully about the role model that we present. Our own shortcomings may be reflected in our children! Many teachers will tell you that meeting a child's parents at the first parent teacher evening of the year is often a revelation that explains much about the child and their character traits.

On more than one occasion I've struggled to keep a straight face as the parent of a child, summoned to the school because of the child's use of inappropriate language, has said to me 'The little b*****! I don't know where he ******* gets it from. Come here, you little b******!'

So what is our role model for our children – are we teaching them to play the right tunes in life?

Taking a solo: the art of improvisation
Musical improvisation is in some respects an intriguing contradiction. While it is all about making things up as we go along, nevertheless the soloist still has to work within a structure.

You have to listen to the basic rhythm and keep in time while at the same time listening to the bass and chords and staying in harmony, so that the note being played doesn't clash (although occasionally you can add notes called 'passing notes' which don't fit in with a chord, but are quickly OK and can add colour and interest). Improvisation also has to work around the same 'mode' (type of scale).

We all have moments when we want to solo – we want to stand out from the crowd and make our own mark and this is particularly the case during the teenage years. But even teenagers need the underpinning of the family unit with its structure and values in order to improvise successfully. There may well be 'passing notes' but these help to build character. And when the soloist has run out of steam, the band needs to be there to pick up the tune again and keep the music going.

Playing together: tuning, balance and dynamics
With all the elements of the band in place it's important to keep listening – to try to play the right notes, to listen to the rhythm and to stay in tune! The best music is created when everyone listens to each other and respects each other's role.

Being a family is about working together – we need good working relationships with our children. If we can get those relationships right we will have a high quality of family life. As an adjudicator at a music festival once said to the concert band my daughters were playing in – 'Keep checking your tuning! If your instrument is out of tune with the rest of the band, then every note you play is a wrong note.' Our lives are often lived at such a pace that sometimes we carry on, regardless of the wider picture, perhaps not aware that what we are doing is out of tune with everyone else, and causing discordance.

And so every now and then it is a good idea to stop and check our tuning – both individually and as a family! This could involve standing back from family life and reflecting, and perhaps making some small (or even major) adjustments. It could be you that is out of tune – or the others in the band. (Sometimes it's too easy to think that others are out of tune and that we're the only instrument that isn't!) From time to time we may need to stop our children and help them to re-tune. It may just have been a minor wrong note, played by mistake – or it might need a complete re-tune. This 're-tuning' will, of course, be based on discussion – and the more able both children and parents are to talk about issues, the better. (See the following chapter, where Roy offers a wealth of exercises for developing communication within the family.) I heard recently of a family in which the father (who is a business manager) holds an 'AGM' with his young child, where they 'review' recent incidents and discuss how the child feels about the parenting he is receiving – and how it could be improved! As well as giving the child an opportunity to express his feelings about his role within the family, it also gives the father a chance to explain why there are certain rules!

While this may not work for all families, the opportunity for discussion and openness and the time spent considering each other's viewpoint has to be a positive. It is important however that this consultation is not allowed to undermine the parent's ultimate authority within the family. As with all family dynamics, it is about getting the balance right. As Sue Palmer writes, it is essential to be authoritative without being authoritarian; with authority comes responsibility.

... And the band plays on

The personnel of a band can often change; members can sometimes leave and new ones be recruited. This has many parallels with the fluidity of the modern family unit. Relationships change the dynamics: older children move away, some bring new members in (boyfriends/girlfriends, husbands/wives), some are lost forever. But we should not see these as a threat, merely a chance to broaden horizons; an opportunity to embrace the changes and make new music.

Eventually, equipped with the skills and influences they've acquired in our 'family bands', our children will be able to form a band of their own!

Footnotes and further reading

1. Palmer, Sue (2006), *Toxic Childhood: How the Modern World Is Damaging Our Children and What We Can Do About it*. London: Orion.

2. Wikipedia *Music and the Brain: 9 Auditory Cortices*

3. On Children, from *The Prophet* by Kahil Gibran.

4. Sheppard, Philip (2005), *Music Makes your Child Smarter*. Beaconsfield: Artemis Music.

5. Frostick, Richard, Music teacher quoted in BBC online *Parents' Music Room* www.bbc.co.uk/music/parents/learninganinstrument.

6. Palmer, Sue (2006), *Toxic Childhood: How the Modern World Is Damaging Our Children and What We Can Do About it*. London: Orion.

7. Moore, D. G., Burland, K. and Davidson, J. W. W. (2003), 'The social context of musical success: A developmental account'. *British Journal of Psychology*, 94.

8. Sheppard, Philip (2005), *Music Makes your Child Smarter*. Beaconsfield: Artemis Music.

9. Tramo, Mark, quoted in Cromie, William J., *How Your Brain Listens to Music. Harvard University Gazette*, 13 November 1997, www.hno.harvard.edu/gazette/1997/11.13/HowYourBrainLis.html.

10. www.edu-cyberpg.com/Music/morebrain.html quoting from The Psychology of Music, 24 (2).

11. DfES (2007), *Letters and Sounds: Principles and Practice of High Quality Phonics*. London: HMSO.

12. Hohmann, Mary and Weikart, David T. (1995), *Educating Young Children*. Michigan: High/Scope Educational Research Foundation Ypsilanti.

13. Lamont, Alexandra, Lecturer in the Psychology of Music at the University of Keele quoted in BBC online *Parents' Music Room*: www.bbc.co.uk/music/parents/yourchild/why_musicmatters.shtml.

14. Moran, Caitlin (2007), *Knowledge* magazine, *The Times* August 18–24.

15. www.suzukiassociation.org.

16. Farman, John (2005) *Bringing Up your Parents: A Guide for Teenagers* (Revised edition). London: Piccadilly Press.

17. www.artscouncil.org.uk.

18. *Sound on Sound* magazine, November 2003.

19. Palmer, Sue (2006), *Toxic Childhood: How the Modern World Is Damaging Our Children and What We Can Do About it*. London: Orion.

Introducing Roy Leighton – *by Jim Houghton*

Roy is a fascinating character, an inspirational speaker and a deep thinker who has built on his acting skills to become a coach and guide to students, teachers, managers and leaders in all walks of life, working at local, national and international level. He is also a member of an inspirational group of educational presenters who work collectively through an organization called Independent Thinking Ltd, with the strap line: 'Do things no-one does or do things everyone does in a way no-one does.'

Roy believes that the four domains of intellectual, emotional, practical and spiritual development are key not only for our children, but are also an important focus for us as adults. And again, it is not about arriving at a destination, but realizing that this is a journey of continuous refinement for all of us. Fundamentally, he argues that if we want our children to develop in the four domains above, we, as parents and carers, need to show that we are continuing to develop too. On the back of this thinking he offers a number of exercises for families to engage in to help all the members to balance the driving influence of our evolving view of the world with that of our behaviour and thinking.

He bases these ideas on the work of Dr Clare Graves, who established a theory of the emerging levels of human existence from survival through to interdependence. Although founded on this research, the actual exercises for the family are really straightforward and accessible. This chapter fundamentally sets out to provide a number of tools and exercises that will help your family to become more tolerant, supportive and appreciative. And of course the content of the previous three chapters can collectively provide the media of drama, story and music as vehicles for these aspirations.

In essence, this whole book is based on the precept that families are the glue of society: the authors set out to propose that by positive, creative actions the collective force of the family can be steered to help us all become more fulfilled and effective people whatever stage we are in life. The wealth of ideas and activities from all the authors, but brought together in this chapter by Roy, make up a powerful resource to build truly happy families.

chapter **four**

Act your age!:
The path to maturity

'There is an Indian proverb or axiom that says that everyone is a house with four rooms; a physical, a mental, an emotional and a spiritual. Most of us tend to live in one room most of the time but unless we go into every room every day, even if only to keep it aired, we are not a complete person.'

Rumer Godden: 'The House with Four Rooms'

I have, since 1982, been on a personal and professional journey with teachers, students, business people, communities, politicians and a variety of professionals to help them (and myself) to create environments where people function at a level of evolution needed to effectively fulfil their roles. The exercises that accompany each section in this book will assist you to further develop the vital skills of being a real 'grown-up'. I do not believe that this journey will ever end. As Dr Clare W. Graves, whose work forms the basis for this chapter, said in his explanation of how a human being evolves:

'As he [or she] sets off on each quest, he believes he will find the answer to his existence, and as he settles into each nodal state he is certain he has found it. Yet, always to his surprise and ever to his dismay he finds, at every stage, that the solution to existence is not the solution he thinks he has found. Every state he reaches leaves him discontented and perplexed. It is simply that as he solves one set of human problems, he finds a new set in their place. The quest he finds is never-ending.'[1]

It was when I had the good fortune to meet and undergo training in Gravesian methodology with Chris Cowan (a friend and colleague of Graves) and Natasha Todorovic[2] that I believe I was provided with the key to unlocking and gaining access to my own mature adult self. This may seem a huge statement, but I believe it is justified – as, hopefully, the following will show.

Over the past few years I have used Gravesian ideas to provide a framework for reflection, understanding and practical action. It is a fascinating journey and one that I would like to share with you in the hope that it can assist you in managing the next stage of your personal evolution and to provide you with strategies to support the development of the people, particularly your family and the children who are in your care.

What does an adult look like?

Clare W. Graves was a psychologist working in America from the 1940s through to the 1970s who found himself frustrated by the various opinions and theories to do with defining 'the mature adult personality'. He wanted to provide a clearer path for analysis of human development without generating complexity where there need not be any, or introducing simplicity to aspects of human behaviour that were genuinely complex. He wondered why so many viewpoints could exist – all with a measure of truth – yet none suitable for all cases. Graves looked for something to wrap them all together and break through the confusion of overlapping views of human nature and learning.

It was this confusion that drove him in his research and ultimately provided us with a language of maturity that can readily form the basis of more complex ideas, debates and actions. To show this journey Graves presented the flow, expansion and dynamic shifting process of human evolution in the form of a double helix (see Figure 1). This drawing also has a simple reference point using letters of the alphabet (see the table summarizing these levels on page 105 for a short explanation of how the letters were used). The image subsequently came to be represented by a spiral (see Figure 2), hence the later term for his approach 'Spiral Dynamics'. The spiral shows how each stage of evolution embraces earlier stages and develops its own uniqueness only to be absorbed itself by the next emerging level. Graves' original diagram (Figure 1) shows the emergence of this image.

The double helix shows the two driving influences on our world views; one being our internal neurology (thinking and psychology) and the other our external social and environmental conditions. In other words: we may change our thinking or our actions if something changes in our world, and we may change how we see our world if we are exposed to new ideas that challenge how we think or act. I say 'may' not necessarily 'will' as, in many cases, even when the reality of our shifting world and new information challenges where we are and what we are doing, many of us hold onto a world that we are comfortable with, even if it is no longer true, real or helpful. It's the friction between life conditions and mind capacities that generates a world view, resulting in behaviour that fits that kind of world. We try to find balance between how we think and the world we are in.

Steve, Tim and Trish, in their earlier chapters, all highlight the need for being open to the stories of others and the changes around us. This final chapter will provide a clear framework for understanding and applying the key messages and exercises highlighted throughout this book.

Movement along the spiral happens when the problems in our world change or how we think about them changes. It is important to note that no one level is better than another. We all move up and down the levels as our circumstances change. Sometimes one fits better than others. Moving up is about inhabiting more psychological space as our world changes and we respond to it. That gives us more flexibility to live in a complicated world.

Graves made this point clear when he said:

> 'I am not saying in this conception of adult behaviour that one style of being, one form of human existence is inevitably and in all circumstances superior to or better than another form of human existence, another style of being. What I am saying is that when one form of being is more congruent with the realities of existence, then it is the better form of living for those realities. And what I am saying is that when one form of existence ceases to be functional for the realities of existence then some other form, either higher or lower in the hierarchy, is the better form of living. I do suggest, however, and this I deeply believe is so, that for the overall welfare of total man's existence in this world, over the long run of time, higher levels are better than lower levels and that the prime good of any society's governing figures should be to promote human movement up the levels of human existence.'

If we want our children and families as a whole to evolve, then the best way to achieve this is for us as parents, partners and siblings to be a living example of evolution in action. If we have stopped, why should the children around us start? If we don't take responsibility for our own development, as 'adults' we will find it hard to support and the development in others.

> 'Imagine life as a game in which you are juggling five balls in the air. You name them – work, family, health, friends, and spirit – and you're keeping all of these in the air. You will soon understand that work is a rubber ball. If you drop it, it will bounce back. But the other four balls – family, health, friends, and spirit are made of glass. If you drop one of these, they will be irrevocably scuffed, marked, nicked, damaged, or even shattered. They will never be the same. You must understand that and strive for balance in your life.' (Brian Dyson, CEO of Coca Cola (1994))

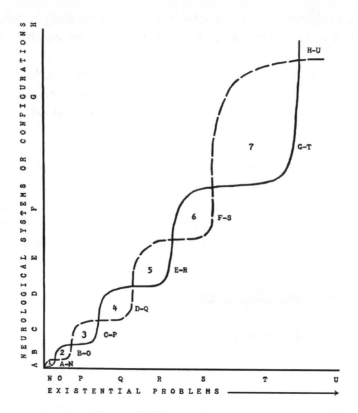

Fig. 1

Alvin Toffler, educator and visionary, said in his apocryphal 1970s work[4] *Future Shock* that:

> 'The illiterate of the 21st Century will not be those people that cannot read or write, but those who cannot learn, unlearn and relearn.'

We now find ourselves in the future that he predicted and see that his words were chillingly accurate. Why are there growing numbers of 'educated' and 'qualified' young people leaving schools with qualifications but lacking basic social or 'life' skills that are needed in the work place? What is it that businesses and university departments demand that these young people are lacking? How many people do you know who are 'qualified' but lack the basic competences to move their theory into action?

Fig. 2[3]

Learning for the 21st Century, a report from a new public-private coalition known as the Partnership for 21st Century Skills (www.21stcenturyskills.org), provides a framework for educators, policy-holders and parents to show how schools can prepare students to succeed in the first decades of the twenty-first century.

> 'To cope with the demands of the 21st century, students need to know more than core subjects. They need to know how to use their knowledge and skills by thinking critically, applying knowledge to new situations, analysing information, comprehending new ideas, communicating, collaborating, solving problems, and making decisions.'[5]

Qualifications are certainly a key aspect of the selection process (I imagine they always will be), but qualifications alone are not enough. If we are to support our children to develop the skills needed to survive the twenty-first century then we need to develop a multiply intelligent and emotionally mature generation – not just people who can pass exams.

Like Toffler, Graves' hunch was that humans had to learn to embrace change in order to grow. He wanted to provide a 'system' that could be understood and used as the basis for clear communication with others interested and working in the field of human psychological evolution.

These levels of human existence will be presented in order of development and at each level provide some practical activities for your own personal development and that of your whole family. Graves talks about the transitions between levels from a 'me'- to a 'we'- centred existence. Some of us prefer to see a world that is either 'selfish' or 'selfless'. We need both. A balance between working for the benefit of self and others – and not either/or – is the essence of maturity. Professor Charles Handy sums up this need for balance in life and work as 'proper selfishness'.[6] Again, the double helix is a good image to bear in mind for this transition process from 'me' to 'we'.

Finally, before we investigate the levels in more detail, bear in mind the earlier point that none of the levels of the spiral are 'better' than others. All are needed as you, your environment and the people you are with shift, change and evolve. When we seek to freeze ourselves into an absolute view of the world, we become inflexible and stilted in our growth. We need all of the levels to adjust and engage in the constantly varying world of which we are not only a part but influence, and are influenced by, day by day and moment by moment.

When development gets blocked, it is not where we are on the spiral, but whether we are 'open' or 'closed'. When we get to a level where we are comfortable, we run the risk of getting stuck and closing ourselves off to the other states when this one world view and set of behaviours works for us (or at least makes us feel balanced, safe and secure). If we can remain open, we have more options to adapt.

This is further reinforced if we surround ourselves with others who have a shared 'closed' world view. Strength in numbers means that our thinking and behaviour are reinforced and therefore must be the 'right way'. This can lead to huge – even violent – resistance to the ideas, opinions and activities of others who are not part of this intimate group, family or society.

At the limit of this lurks extremism – people choosing to act in such a way as to be totally closed to the ideas, actions and feelings of others. As a parent, one of my desires – and one of the driving forces for me agreeing to contribute to this book – is that I wish my children to be part of the generation that is dominated by grown-ups: intelligent, articulate, compassionate, practical human beings who would never contemplate harming others merely because someone may choose to look at the world from a different place to themselves.

If we are to assist our children to have a balanced and enjoyable adulthood we, as the adults that form the society they look to for signals and signs of 'acceptable' behaviour, need to have the courage and confidence to go regularly into the four rooms that Rumer Godden refers to in the passage at the start of this chapter. To simply take refuge in one room is to present an impartial view of the world to those very people who need to see the complexity and potential of a world that they will, eventually, be responsible for.

The safest and most dynamic environment to support this process is the family unit. As you have read in the earlier passages, and will see in the following pages, for a group of people drawn together by apparent chance to become a real family requires many qualities including: openness, innovation, enterprise and the ability to constantly change and evolve.

Graves split the alphabet into two as a quick reference point to show the emerging states. A to M shows the developing world view (neurological systems or configurations as Graves first put it); N to Z shows the corresponding thinking and behaviour (or existential problems). We have not used all the letters of the alphabet as this is an evolutionary model and we are still evolving.

A summary of the Gravesian Levels of Human Existence

World view		Level Of Human Existence	Thinking/Behaviour	
H	All things are dependent on each other for survival	Interdependent	Global, holistic	U
G	The world is complex	Interconnected	Systems thinking	T
F	We are all equal	Community	Empathy, collaboration	S
E	Full of opportunities	Enterprise	Working for personal reward in the medium and long term	R
D	The world is in chaos	Order	Hierarchy, rules, structure	Q
C	Only the strong survive	Self	Impulsive, power, instant gain	P
B	Unsafe, mysterious, strange forces around us	Tribal	Family, icons, rituals	0
A	No world view at this level	Survival	Eat, sleep, sex	N

Survival

'Your children are not your children.

They are the sons and daughters of Life's longing for itself.'

Kahlil Gibran, The Prophet

A new-born baby will focus on survival in the form of sustenance and sleep. This is seen by many as the most crucial stage of evolution. At this stage our neurological and existential development is centred on survival and there is no such thing as a world view.

None of the states are fixed and survival is no exception. Once we are past the first few months of childhood, survival doesn't become the dominant state for the majority of us. If we do find ourselves back at this point it will be due to some dramatic shift in our world or our thinking that flings us back to this most basic of conditions. Grieving, fear or loss can propel us back to using survival strategies where we can only exist by getting through each day or even each moment.

This first level of a child's development is 'me' centred. Neurologically, intellectually, emotionally, practically and intuitively they have not formed a relationship with the world around them. It is the role of the other family members to protect, provide and support them until they can make a more conscious effort to the happiness of others. Their very presence tends, in most cases, to provide inspiration and an outpouring of love for most. However, this is not a planned strategy on their part. They just happen to be cute and all that love towards them from others is a reflex action. To maintain this ability to generate spontaneous love and affection from others as we get older requires greater effort. While this chapter is not about being able to call forth cooing and kissing from all that meet us it will provide some practical activities for supporting the individual and collective development of the whole family. Cooing and kissing are an optional extra.

> 'What can you do to promote world peace? Go home and love your family' Mother Teresa

At each level there are exercises that we can do with our children and ones that we can do for ourselves. Exercises for children can be adapted as we all have children of varying ages so we need to be a bit flexible. However, the exercises for yourself should be taken in order. Regard these as a step-by-step review and development process for your own evolution. Do not be tempted to leap a level! Work through them in order – there is a planned process and the impact of later exercises is dependent on your application and reflection of earlier ones.

Survival exercise for 'me'

What gets me going? – Getting back to basics as a parent/adult is always a good thing to do – just to check that we are grounded and have a foundation to build a secure self from. Think of it as airing your four rooms of intellect, emotion, practicality and spirituality. The challenge in this exercise is that it may reveal that our foundation needs a bit of 'underpinning'. As mentioned earlier, Graves talks about our 'locus of control' or point of influence being 'me'- or 'we'-centred – both have positive and negative possibilities. As you complete these exercises, notice if you become more 'open' or 'closed' in your thinking. Your response will be a good indicator as to how you react to the thoughts, feelings and actions of others. Obviously this book is highlighting how we respond to the children and family members in our care, but the exercises will also give you a chance to reflect on the relationships with all the people around you. Family or not.

So, let's do a survival check!

Get a pen and paper and put aside some time (20 minutes or so) when you can focus on this task.

Write down the question 'Why am I here?' at the top of the page then, without spending too much time pondering, write down a list of possible answers. Keep on writing until you have come up with at least 25 points. I would suggest you put the book down now and complete the exercise before continuing with this chapter. Not essential but recommended!

When you have finished, review the list and then note if the answers are 'me' centred ('I am here to look after myself') or 'we' centred ('I am here to make a positive contribution to my family/society'). After going through the list, do you see a dominant pattern? Are you more 'me' than 'we', or vice-versa? Is it balanced or out-of-kilter?

Whatever the outcome, reflect on the list and then share your findings with a friend, family member or an older child (12+). After discussing any recurrent themes, write down on a fresh piece of paper a goal, statement or intention that sums up your direction or desire for the next 100 days. For example, 'I am going to have more fun with my family' or 'I am going to learn Spanish', 'I am going to exercise three times a week so I feel good about how I look and feel'. Make the wording of your statement 'me' focused and positive. No 'try' or 'would like', thank you very much. Write down on the page the date that marks the 100th day.

Your goal now is to read this statement each morning and to take action every day, for yourself, to create a world where you, the people around you and the environment where you live and work support this. One of the most powerful aids to developing the courage, compassion and capacity of our children as they move towards maturity is our own example. Not necessarily our successes – rather our examples of tenacity, tolerance and resilience when we encounter set-backs and failure. Mahatma Gandhi summed up this attitude when he said that we should 'be the change we want to see in the world'.

To help our children move effectively through all the levels they need to see that we as parents have not got to a point of stagnation. If they perceive that adulthood is a destination rather than a process they will forever search for a place where they can stop. It is important they realize that, as adults, once we have solved one set of problems, we need to prepare ourselves to manage bigger challenges that inevitably manifest themselves in our lives. Life is a struggle. This is the reality. Suffering through this struggle is optional.

Survival exercise for 'we'

Touch time – The focus for babies is safety and sustenance so that must be your focus as a parent. Make sure they are clean, warm and loved. At this level of human existence children need lots of touch, eye contact, love and stimulation.

The levels of human existence, as stated earlier, are a combination of neurological and existential development and so the focus here is to 'grow their brain' by stimulating all of the senses. A child's brain develops at a staggering rate in the first few years of its life. This wiring up process continues all our lives but we develop a 'mature' brain around 25 years old. Our emotional maturity is directly linked to the capacity of us to assist in the 'maturation' of our brain. This amazing process is driven by the primary role of the brain which is to assist us in our survival. A baby, from the moment it arrives in this world is seeking to make sense of it. The wiring up of our brain means that child can grow into a thinking, feeling, aware individual that can survive in the world.

It's our job as parents to create the conditions within the family for this to happen[7]. When appropriate stimulation and engagement does not occur in these formative months and years the impact on the development of the brain and subsequent emotional and intellectual abilities of the child can last a lifetime. Create an environment for your baby to have sounds, sights, smells, touch and tastes that stimulate.

In this exercise the focus is on the physical interaction between children and their parents. There is a clear link between safe and appropriate physical contact with a baby and their brain development. The tragic experience of babies in Romania who were 'housed' in some of the orphanages highlights what can happen when babies aren't supported through the 'survival' stage of neurological development.

These babies were put in mini prison cells – cots stacked one on top of another – and only taken out for changing and feeding. Charles A. Nelson, council member for the National Scientific Council on the Developing Child, highlights the impact of this treatment on their development:

'In virtually every aspect of development we've looked at – cognition, brain development, social-emotional development, physical development, language – institutionalisation negatively affects development in profound ways.'[8]

This is an extreme example but is shown to highlight the importance of assisting the development of the brain through regular safe and loving interactions with others.

Having bathed your child, place the child on a towel or soft cloth in a warm room and gently apply baby lotion or oil. Take your time over this. Remember that your aim is to connect physically and emotionally with your baby. Play music that is relaxing. It doesn't have to be classical or too highbrow, just something that makes you feel calm – if you feel good this will be picked up and responded to by your child.

Spend a few minutes doing this. I would suggest doing it at the same time every day to help establish ritual and order. Children need to develop routine and ritual – it makes them feel safe.

This is an exercise that can be adapted throughout your time with your children at whatever age. Obviously the level of massage and physical contact will need to be appropriate to the age and sex of the child, but be sure to keep in contact with your children. This can take the form of sport, holding hands, hugging, playing or dancing. We have, certainly in the West, a very unbalanced approach when it comes to physical contact with our children.

Psychologist Sylvia Clare supports this point:

> 'The experiences a child receives throughout their life shape the way their brains develop. Children who do not receive sufficient appropriate touch are unable to form important neural connections. This leads to their becoming desensitised. The result can be an inability to engage in physical touch without experiencing acute discomfort or even pain. Such children are likely to develop into people lacking in empathy, emotional warmth and the basic ability to engage in normal human adult relationships ... When I worked as a school counselor, I helped the children I worked with understand these differences where appropriate. They understood what was meant instinctively and without any need for any threatening or graphic descriptions of what might ensue. They just knew that some things felt good and some didn't. They learned to trust that intuitive knowledge in themselves.
>
> My decision was to ignore these guidelines and make appropriate contact with the children I saw, even when alone with them, because some of them had such heartbreaking stories to share and I was so much more able to help them and develop a trusting relationship as a result. I decided to take a risk of being accused of something, knowing in my own heart and mind that all I felt was deep human compassion. I trusted that my motivations alone would protect me from any threats of litigation and claims of professional misconduct.'[9]

How many great parents do not get close to their children physically because they are fearful of being labelled a paedophile? This is particularly, but not exclusively, the domain of men. Steve Biddulph highlights this issue in his excellent book *Raising Boys* when he says: 'If you want to get along with boys, learn how to wrestle.'

Why? Well, in brief:

● Baby boys are born with the same amount of testosterone as a 12-year-old boy! The testosterone levels settle down, but will peak again around 3–4 years.

Testosterone levels will continue to go up and down and by the age of 11–14 will rise by 800 per cent.

- The surge in testosterone slows down connections to the language part of the brain. It also makes them more muscular, active, restless, argumentative, impulsive and disorganized. They need to have a clear set of rules or they will be prone to disorder, disengagement and depression.

- From 6–13 boys are learning how to be male and they start to 'lock onto Dad' to study how to act, talk, and be 'a real man'. That window of time is the biggest opportunity for fathers to have an influence on their sons.

- When boys are play-wrestling with each other and their parents (particularly Dad) they are actually learning about their bodies, strength and limits.

Knowing power, knowing when to stop and being able to manage the drive to go 'too far' is a lesson that needs to be learnt early on in boys. The implications of not managing this physical and violent power in boys can lead to macho and dominant behaviour in our relationships at home and work. How many men do you know who find it hard to control their physical impulses or who get 'physical' when they feel they are challenged intellectually or emotionally? Hence Stephen Biddulph's advice, which is particularly, but not exclusively, aimed at fathers.

Physical and emotional closeness needs to start early and continue throughout our lives. This development of the awareness of physical power and strength, balanced with the emotional capacity to temper it and not be driven by 'tribal'- or even 'survival'-centred existence will support our children to become balanced adults. It will also assist our boys in becoming 'real men'.

The film director Kevin Smith has this to say on the matter, which I'm sure would make his dad proud:

> 'My father taught me how to be a man – and not by instilling in me a sense of machismo or an agenda of dominance. He taught me that a real man doesn't take, he gives; he doesn't use force, he uses logic; doesn't play the role of trouble-maker, but rather, trouble-shooter; and most importantly, a real man is defined by what's in his heart, not his pants.'

Tribal

'There's one sad truth in life I've found

While journeying east and west –

The only folks we really wound

Are those we love the best.

We flatter those we scarcely know,

We please the fleeting guest,

And deal full many a thoughtless blow

To those who love us best.'

Ella Wheeler Wilcox

From around 4 months old, a baby is becoming aware that they are part of (but not separate from) the world. They know that there are strange and powerful forces beyond them that they do not understand. Certain images (parents' faces, a favourite toy, their own hand, etc.) are becoming more recognizable, and provide reassurance and comfort. This world view impacts their behaviour – they know if they cry the strange God-like creature (the parent and most often the mother) will come to hold and feed them. They are moving from a 'me'- to a 'we'-centred view of the world. They are becoming aware that they are linked to things, people and objects outside themselves.

Obviously this mindset can also impact adults and groups. If we perceive another person or group as a threat we can quickly resort to negative tribal behaviour. A modern-day tribal state that can be both positive and negative is football. Positive in that it brings together a group with a shared view of the world. Their uniform and images (football strip) and icons (footballers, stadium, etc.) help to give them a collective identity. Importantly, this is an identity that is different to another group.

A closed tribal state might say 'because you support a team that wears blue and my team wear red then you must be a threat because you're different'. When we are threatened, we trip a gland in the brain called the amygdala, which then floods the body with chemicals and causes us to respond at a very tribal level. We may be driven to react in one of four ways: fight, flight, freeze or flock.

When confronted with a perceived threat from another group, unless we are consciously aware of what is happening to us neurologically, we run the risk of responding inappropriately because we are being dragged into a tribal or even survival state. When cultures are embedded in a highly charged and extreme tribal state they can end up with persecution, imprisonment and murder. It's important to note that, just because we have an emotional reaction to something, this does not mean we are justified in acting on this emotion. Aristotle highlighted this challenge of managing our emotional state when he said:

> 'Anybody can become angry – that is easy, but to be angry with the right person and to the right degree and at the right time and for the right purpose, and in the right way – that is not within everybody's power and is not easy.'

Being a 4 month old in this state is acceptable, but responding in this way as an adult is not in most situations. Would it not be a real testimony to our capacity to learn, and a legacy for future generations, if we could support our children to truly evolve to be intellectually, emotionally, practically and spiritually mature adults? What would the impact on the world be? Well, for that to happen we need to come back to our own tribal behaviour.

Tribal exercise for 'me'

What do you think of me? – As parents, we need a network of support. Traditionally that has been the immediate family, but with contemporary notions of a family unit, this will vary. The key point here is: do you have a tribe that can assist you? An African proverb states that 'it takes a whole village to raise a child'. So, who is your tribe? Choose at least three people (family and friends/neighbours) whom you trust to speak the truth to you. Real friends who are not just going to say what they think you want to hear. You may prime them for this exercise in positive tribal support by sharing the following Japanese axiom:

> 'If you befriend someone, but lack the courage to correct them, you are, in fact, their enemy.'

Grab a pen and paper and sit yourself down with a friend or family member in a place where you can talk and not be disturbed. You are going to ask them three questions, then listen to what they say. Crucially this means you do not seek to interrupt, explain, challenge, apologize or question. You can only say 'thank you' or encourage them to be more open; 'I appreciate this, do go on', etc. Write down some of the key points – this will be a means of remembering and you can return to the notes at a later stage.

First question: What are my strengths and best qualities?
Second question: What are my areas for development/weaknesses?
Third question: How can I be more aware of the impact I am having on others?

Listen to the feedback, thank whoever you are speaking to and, even though you might want to respond, resist the temptation! Leave it for 24 hours and sleep on it before going back to comment.

When you have spoken to everyone, review what's been said and see if there are any key messages that have cropped up more than once. If there are, you have a choice: ignore the message from the tribe or seek help from the tribe to challenge your own behaviour/

patterns. This will require further conversation and possibly you requesting help. The positive aspect of the tribe is that it is there to help you, even if it does not agree with your actions from time to time.

Tribal exercise for 'we'

Head of the table – One game that has evolved in my family is this one. It encourages everyone to have a voice and everyone else to actively listen. It means that meal times are more than just eating but a time for catching up with each other.

> 'Nothing would be more tiresome than eating and drinking if God had not made them a pleasure as well as a necessity.' Voltaire

One fundamental tribal activity is sharing food together. A family that does not make effort to engage and utilize the ritual of meal times runs a serious risk of building a house full of individuals who see their needs, their dreams and their challenges and fears as something to deal with on their own and not as part of the tribe. This could lead to a family who individually feel alone and unable to communicate their joys and sorrows to anyone else. The family is the rehearsal space for interaction with the world outside the home. Unless time is spent developing these essential group (tribal) skills in the safety of a family then this can, and often does, lead to misunderstandings in future relationships both at home and work. Think of your own childhood and ask yourself if you 'survived' or 'celebrated' meal times? Was the sharing of food and time a blessing or a curse?

There have been many enlightening and important things that have come to light using this simple and fun activity. Around the age of 7 my middle daughter, Ellie, revealed that she was being bullied at school. As we regularly listen to each other we were able to deal with this before it became a serious issue (for both Ellie and the bully). Had we left this for even a few more weeks and not discovered what was happening it may well have moved into a pattern of victimization that would have been much harder to manage.

Do not be fooled by the simple nature of this and many of the examples that I will give. Underlying these tasks lie sound theory and practical experience. Simple does not mean simplistic. So, let us begin and, as Einstein said: Make everything as simple as possible, but not simpler.

First choose who is going to be head of the table. Make sure that over the days and weeks everyone has a turn at being head. Positive 'tribal' means that there is a close hierarchy where people support, listen and obey the rules for the good of the tribe. Again, I cannot overstate the importance of making sure that the positive aspects of tribal will provide us with the support, confidence and love throughout our lives for when we have to deal with greater and greater challenges.

The head of the table chooses a question to put to the rest of the family and then decides the order in which people contribute. The questions should encourage people to talk about their day (or week) such as: 'What has made you happy and what has made you sad?'; 'What have you done that was a challenge and how did it make you feel?', etc.

Everyone speaks without interruption and everyone else listens. Allow unlimited time for everyone to speak, or if time is precious, give each person the same amount of time with a 30-second warning to finish from the head of the table. The head of the table talks last.

By engaging in this exercise regularly (at least once a week) a family will develop skills of listening, reflection, empathy, problem solving, emotional intelligence and patience. This foundation should be returned to again and again as it is the essence of a family that can develop individuals who can function in a supportive, selfless and harmonious way. And it is this transcendence from the 'tribe' to 'self' that is our next challenge along the journey of evolution.

Self

'The young child is totally egocentric – meaning not that he thinks selfishly only about himself, but on the contrary, that he is incapable of thinking about himself. The egocentric child is unable to differentiate himself from the rest of the world: he has not separated himself out from others or from objects. Thus he feels that others share his pain or his pleasure, that his mumblings will inevitably be understood, that his perspective is shared by all persons, that even animals and plants partake of his consciousness. In playing hide-and-seek he will "hide" in broad view of other persons, because his egocentrism prevents him from recognizing that others are aware of his location. The whole course of human development can be viewed as a continuing decline of egocentrism.' Howard Gardner

This is a tricky stage and, in my experience, the level where most of us find it hardest to move on from. We want our children to become independent and to have a positive sense of self. We also want them to be able to work effectively alongside each other and be able to communicate and manage conflicts that will inevitably arise. At some point, usually during puberty, they are developing this sense of self in independence and will challenge our values and ways of seeing the world. This is a good thing – if they didn't find some motivation for moving from a world they have out-grown (our world) they would want to live with us forever! But let us hold fire on the puberty stage for a while and go back a few years.

At around 2 or 3 years old (the terrible twos), a child begins developing the realization that they have influence and impact on the world. Cause and effect take on a very concrete reality. They know that pushing 'this' causes 'that' to fall over. If they want the attention of their parents they have a variety of tools to bring the focus back to them. Also, for boys (back to Biddulph) they are experiencing a massive surge in testosterone levels and unless they have clear rules, guidelines and instructions they can easily get confused, agitated and frustrated.

Remember the double helix – me, we, me, we, etc. They are now moving from 'we'/tribal – part of the whole, to the 'me'/self – impulsive and dynamic. Immediate gratification – emotionally, physically, intuitively or intellectually – is a huge driver at this stage of development.

At this crucial age children are becoming aware of this *'trauma of transition'*. They have to start managing their transition, yet they are unable or unwilling to take responsibility for their actions and reactions when they realize that the rest of the world won't play ball with their egocentricity. Having had a few years of protection, love and support and sometimes the message from their parents that they are the centre of the universe, it can come as a shock to find out that they are not.

'It is not easy to find happiness in ourselves, and it is not possible to find it elsewhere.' Agnes Repplier

This lesson, in many cases, is never fully learnt by a fair few 'grown-ups'. How many people do you know who, when they don't get what they want, abandon logical argument and reason and go into 'chucking teddy out of the pram' state?

As a family, and particularly as the 'elders' within the family we need not only to seek to understand this constant evolutionary process but to guide our children to a future that will make sense to them. Alvin Toffler highlights this point when he says: 'Our moral responsibility is not to stop the future, but to shape it ... to channel our destiny in humane directions and to try to ease the trauma of transition.' [10]

If we assist our children in navigating this level we will achieve much in helping their long-term happiness and success as people.

Self exercise for 'me'

Becoming a centred self and not self-centred – Following on from the tribal exercise, take one thing that your friends and family have said about you that would make you happier and do it or begin it.

It could be anything from booking yourself in for a massage or session at the gym or signing up for a night class in Spanish or salsa dancing. Whatever it is, book the time in, pay for it and let everyone know that this is what you are doing and that you want their support.

For those of you reading this that have just responded to that suggestion with the thought 'How am I going to fit this in with everything else I have to do?' let me ask you this: if a family member or friend really needed your help would you give it? If this meant that for a few hours a week you would be there for them to encourage, listen and help them would you do that? If the answer is 'yes' to others but 'no' to yourself then this is your challenge. Imagine you are your own best friend – make the effort for you. Book the time in for and with yourself as if you were as important as anyone else. If you do this, everyone else will gain.

They will gain because they will see the example you are setting and they may also gain by having to manage things in their own life that previously you may have taken on.

Self exercise for 'we'

Dinner table talent – Here is another dinner-time exercise to help develop the positive self of all the family.

The head of the table leads this exercise and chooses one person that the family are going to begin the process of 'bigging-up'.

The question to everyone in the first of this two-stage process is: 'What is great about … ?' And then everyone goes round and says what is great about that family member. Some of the responses from my own family have been: 'They are good at giving hugs', 'They help me when I cannot do something', 'They are a bit mad in a good way', 'They have a great smile', 'They are great at listening to me when I need to talk'.

This exercise tends to work better if you go round the table clockwise (or anti-clockwise) rather than ad hoc. It gives people a clear idea as to whom they are going to compliment and so they have time to think.

Stage 2 of this exercise – best done when everyone has had some positive feedback – is for people to go round the table and say what is great about themselves. This is hugely important. It is not big-headed to say we are good at something. It is not arrogant. The difference between confidence and arrogance is that confident people give you energy and arrogant people steal it. Making our children aware of their own power will stop them feeling the need to drain it from other people.

We all need a positive ego and to know the difference between confidence and arrogance. Saying something positive about oneself is not a crime, but unless we have created the time to hear, regularly, positive statements about who we are and how we are in the world and then to be encouraged to say positive things about ourselves we run the risk of either never feeling good with our success or only feeling good when we have achieved a specific goal. Both extremes are dangerous.

One of the key causes for disharmony, disrespect and disruption in the workplace is the need to cope with people who have never fully formed at this fundamental level of evolution. Let us not add to the disruption and chaos in the world being part of a family dynamic that only produces closed, self-serving individuals that cannot play by any system or set of rules unless they are going to get what they need all the time. In short, let us assist all of our family to be able to function at the next crucial level of evolution: order.

Order

'He who every morning plans the transaction of the day and follows out that plan, carries a thread that will guide him through the maze of the most busy life. But where no plan is laid, where the disposal of time is surrendered merely to the chance of incidence, chaos will soon reign.' Victor Hugo

The need for rules, structure, order and clear processes are hugely helpful, if not vital, for all of us but particularly for young people, especially when moving from childhood into the early stages of puberty, but can cause huge levels of resentment and resistance.

Some children love order and some don't, but the reality is they all need it. Allowing a child to grow into a teenager without providing them with clear parameters is a form of abuse. If we let our children develop a world view where they perceive their needs and wants as central and overriding to everyone else's they run the very high risk of turning into people who have no appreciation for the need for laws and collective responsibility. This will not only impact their success socially, but also academically. They will find it very challenging if they lack the capacity to generate a structure for learning – time-management, self-discipline, independent thinking and research.

I have recently returned from a short visit to Kenya where I worked with children, parents and adults in a remote village four hours drive outside Mombasa. This is a community with very little financial wealth. However, what they lack in money they make up for in personal and collective drive. The children can see that education will help them to improve their social conditions (survival) so they work very well as a community, sharing and supporting each other at many levels (tribal). The children are encouraged to take responsibility for one another and build their own talents (self) and to do this they have a highly disciplined and ordered educational process, with the majority of them seizing every chance they have to improve, learn and develop (order). The driving force here is a need to evolve beyond basic survival. I often have the opposite response when working with young people in the UK.

In the UK I work with secondary school children who go home to three square meals a day (plus snacks), a warm, comfortable house, a TV, a PlayStation, a computer, etc. They may also have parents that 'love' them so much that they get whatever they want. This can generate minutes, hours or possibly days when there is harmony between parent and child. This short-term gratification for both child and parent only fuels a world view that happiness is generated from outside and is in the form of 'stuff' (for the child) or a feeling of low-level recognition and appreciation (for the parent). This is not love. It is emotional bartering.

The 3 year old that got what they wanted from their parents by shouting and being 'a bother' may have learnt that this technique still works at 15. Even worse, the 15 year old that got what they wanted by behaving like this thinks that this is what they then need to do for their kids, otherwise they are not being a good parent. And so the cycle continues.

> 'Civilization begins with order, grows with liberty and dies with chaos.' Will Durant

At some point when we recognize an aspect of our thinking or behaviour that is causing ourselves or others distress, we have the choice to blame other people: parents, society, government or just bad luck. The list goes on. Someone who is 'me' centred and closed to rethinking and re-learning will always find someone else to blame for their unhappiness or lack of success. While it might be true that others are standing in our way, it may also be true that we are using our past experience to justify our lack of action in the present. If we think that this is 'just the way things are' we are probably locked into a closed, rule-bound view of the world and we need to review and move to the next level – enterprise.

Order exercise for 'me'

There is a time and a place – Earlier on in this book Trish talks about the chaos of the morning departure: lost keys, clothes and homework.

In one of those moments that you have begun to schedule in for yourself, get a piece of paper and draw a line down the middle to create two columns. Above the left column write 'out of order' and above the right column write 'put in order'.

Under the 'out of order' column list the things that make mornings mayhem. These may include:

1. Getting myself out of bed.
2. Getting the children out of bed.
3. Making breakfast.
4. Clearing breakfast.
5. Finding homework.
6. Finding shoes.
7. Responding to school requests.

Next, go through and put a suggested solution (put in order) next to the out of order. For example:

1. Buy a loud, old-fashioned alarm clock and put it on the other side of the room.
2. Get them into bed earlier.
3. Set the table the night before (better still, get the children to).
4. Make it part of the jobs that the children help with to earn pocket money. No clearing = no cash.
5. Set things out the night before.
6. Have a place for them and make sure that they are put there as soon as they are taken off.
7. Build in a 'What have you got in your bag today?' every evening.

Take this list to the next family meal or gathering and see what they come up with. This moves the 'me' part of this exercise in to the 'we'.

Order exercise for 'we'

Who moved my keys? – Over the dinner table (preferably after everyone is glowing from their post 'big up' love-in!) present them with the list of what you know needs to be done. At this stage do not share your solutions. This is a 'we' exercise and it is over to them to come up with the solutions.

Present each problem, then go around the table asking people to say how this has a negative impact on themselves and others in the family and ask for a possible solution. Again, keep this as a listening exercise until everyone has spoken before continuing the dialogue about which action to take.

This is a powerful exercise in choice. When children feel they have made a contribution to something and have been genuinely heard then they are more likely to own the new regime. Make an agreement for everyone to all stick to the new timetable/action plan for a week and then review it in a 'head of the table' way at the end of this time.

Once you have agreed the rules, write them up and pop them on the fridge, notice board, toilet or other suitably public family place.

I would also suggest some reward scheme (points or pocket money). When they do the tasks they get credits, when they don't credits are taken away. We do this in our house and it works very well. It teaches cause and effect and the need to take responsibility for being part of a family. They are part of the family, not some non-paying guest.

As potentially boring as rules are if we can see the positive and beneficial gain for self and others then we are more likely to engage. This need for order and personal responsibility was not one that I had much exposure to until I left home. The shock of organizing my own finances and food was frightening.

Get them young is what I say. It is much easier to cope with the challenging teenage years when they are looking for ways of breaking away from the tribe with managed rebellion. This exactly what is to be expected when we shift from 'order' to 'enterprise' during our early teens.

Enterprise

'Man is a goal-seeking animal. His life only has meaning if he is reaching out and striving for his goals.' Aristotle

How often have you heard of the following happening either in your extended family or one that you know of? A young person did very well at primary school. In their final year they were focused and enjoying the experience of being in the classroom. Their grades were good, their behaviour was fine, their attitude to school was positive. In fact they quite like themselves and their achievements and expectations for the future; then off they go to secondary school and within 18 months (if not sooner) it all changes. Their grades have plummeted. They are behaving unreasonably. They have a negative, closed attitude to school, learning becomes a struggle.

This is, of course, a generalization. However, in my work in schools supporting this transition between one learning environment to the next does not, for a huge percentage of our young people, work. At the age of 12, when puberty is kicking in, it is a natural process for young people to move to a more enterprising, self-motivated state and away from externally imposed structures and rules. The next level of learning needs to move them up the spiral, not down. It is there to open them further to challenge and thinking not close them down. This fall-out from learning and the resulting negative shift is very common. The cause? Primary level education is focused on teaching *children* and secondary is focused on teaching *subjects*. Secondary learning, for many, tries to impose too many closed 'order' processes on an emerging generation needing open enterprise. More challenges not less.

The expertise of the vast majority of primary teachers in assisting a child's transition is a joy to watch. It is also extremely complicated to manage the individual learning of a group of 5 year olds. A teacher's ability to keep them collectively focused as well as allowing their individuality to be recognized and celebrated is a real gift.

Primary level education builds the individual learning and life skills from tribal (working with others); on to self (personal confidence and unique skills); then order (understanding rules and taking tests) then onto the next level of human existence – enterprise. This involves taking knowledge and creating something new. By this I mean being able to play by the rules, but being able to come up with new ways of applying old knowledge. It's about encouraging questioning and celebrating challenge and innovation.

Over recent years primary schools around the world have embraced the concept of individual learning and independent thinking, which is the essence of enterprise. As a developing adolescent, using this level positively is a huge opportunity and challenge. Many people – adults and children alike – often regard adolescence as a period of crisis. There are so many changes, challenges and new things to learn. Indeed the Chinese characters for 'crisis' are challenge and opportunity.

The point I am trying to make is that if a child leaves a primary school at a level of maturity that is centred in open enterprise and goes into a learning environment that is working at a lower level of maturity of closed 'order' (structure-led secondary education) there will be a conflict.

I need to just remind us all at this point that each level does not replace the former levels and that every level may be called upon at any time. But – and it is a big but – if the environment does not match and challenge the development of those who are existing in it, the individual will not be able to function effectively.

We have to have rules, but when a child goes from learning using a variety of visual, physical and auditory tools into an environment where the predominant teaching style requires them to passively listen and be lectured at, they cannot learn. A family that is aware of this transition can do much to understand and support the teenagers at home who are finding school tough.

MORI research in the UK compared the delivery style of teachers in secondary schools to the learning style of students.

Out of 24 possible ways of delivering a lesson, the top three delivery styles were: teacher talking, copying from a board or a book and classroom discussion. The three preferred ways of working for the students were: working independently or in small groups on a task, being able to learn by making or moving around and finally being able to listen to music. The MORI research also highlighted that most students are keen to learn, but they are more often than not disengaged.

If we know the learning preference of the children [11] and they are keen to learn, then what is the block? I know I may be sticking my neck out here, but in many cases, it's down to the lack of maturity of some teachers. While I work with some very innovative groups of teachers on some ground-breaking and effective lesson plans, the constant challenge is not 'Does this work?' (IT DOES) but having to deal with the low-level disruption of so-called adults that have got 'their way of doing things' and are closed to implementing any new changes however well researched, effective and well practised elsewhere.

> 'One can have no smaller or greater mastery than mastery of oneself.' Leonardo Da Vinci

Not only teachers. I know that Trish talks earlier about the pain of homework from the parents' point of view. In some cases, we encourage our children to work like us without realizing that they may have different needs to us. By doing this we assume that there is only one way, and that way is our way. Of course, we have to have structure, but if that is all that we have we are not evolving into enterprising individuals. Once we have supported our early teens to enjoy the challenges and gains of enterprise they are then ready to move to the next level. This will take their innovation and 'self'-centred view of the world and see how that can make a positive impact on the wider community.

Enterprise exercise for 'me'

Do you have a 'vision' or an 'illusion'? – Having had time testing your planning and implementation skills with the earlier task of managing the morning rush take this technique one stage further.

This exercise is a great one for challenging limitations of who you are and what you are capable of. It also enables children to start the process of returning the love and support that you have given them.

In one of your quiet moments – that have now become part of your weekly, if not daily, regime – get a piece of paper and create two columns. On top of the first column write 'dreams' on top of the second column write 'action'.

Make a list of all the things you would like to achieve without putting in blocks to achieving them. Keep within the realms of reality. (So, no 'become taller' or 'win the lottery' nonsense.)

Your list might look like:

1. Learn a language.

2. Stop feeling so angry all the time.

3. Be more optimistic.

4. Talk to someone in the family that has been causing me concern.

And so on and so forth.

Do not come up with the solutions, but move straight to the next 'we' exercise.

Enterprise exercise for 'we'

Spot the solution – As with the earlier exercise so with this.

Bring just one dream to the table and ask for help to find practical ways of turning your dream into a reality. This time they need to focus not on just what you need to do but also on what they or others can do to move you closer to your goal.

Rule: if they cannot say something helpful or supportive they say nothing.

When you arrive at the table requesting help from your children (particularly your enterprising teenagers) will more often than not welcome the chance to give advice. Again, this is easing the transition from them being 'children' to taking on the role of 'young adult'.

To develop this further you could encourage them to do the same thing and bring something from their list to the next meal.

Although on a neurological level this exercise is really suited to teenagers and above as it provides them with the opportunity to tell parents and siblings what to do with their lives, it can be fascinating to see younger children approaching what seem, to the 'grown-ups', as huge and insurmountable problems, with a simplicity and directness that is inspiring. Phoebe, my 6 year old, has a perfectly clear view of the world and has brought me back to earth on several occasions with her wisdom and insights.

The innovation and challenge that is found at this level of enterprise is so addictive that many of us get so sucked into it that we run the risk of becoming 'closed'. By this I mean we may find ourselves looking for more personal challenge, gain and 'stuff'. We focus so much on our needs, desires and dreams we can run the risk of never moving to the next level of evolution which takes what we have gained at 'enterprise' to make an impact. We have the chance, if we can move from a closed 'me' to a more open 'we' to use this wealth, both material, creative and intellectual that we amassed at the level of enterprise and add value to the wider community. To influence and support those that are even beyond our family, social group or culture, others that we may not know, understand or even like.

Community

> 'In the third stage of adult-hood, intelligent attention has to be paid not only to one's own advancement and the advancement of the family and society but also to the advancement of the people generally. That too is the responsibility of the grown-ups and they must acquire the skills necessary. They must have wider visions of the peace and prosperity of all mankind, and try to contribute to both, within the limits of their capacity and resources.'
> Sri Sathya Sai Baba

The 'me' to 'we' transition can get more difficult to accept the older we get. We have more control over what we do and the choices we make. Just because we can choose to engage or disengage in an activity does not necessarily mean that we have the capacity to make the right choices. This is even more of a challenge to someone in their mid-teens who is developing physically, neurologically and emotionally at a remarkable rate. They are very likely to be embedded in a 'me'-centred view of the world. This is no bad thing if they are open but, as I highlighted earlier in this chapter, dangerous if closed.

We seem to be constantly hearing of the growing disengagement of young people from the society of which they are part. They want immediate gratification and if they don't get what they want, they act impulsively and for short-term gain. The big block here is the danger of not being able to see the world from other people's points of view. You cannot go from 'me' to a more evolved 'me' without engaging to the right degree with others. Ideally, if we have assisted our children to make effective transitions through the earlier stages then the shift from enterprise to community during mid- to late-teens will prove to be one that they engage in openly, because a tempo for transition has been established in their early years. From an educational perspective this shifting to see their learning and their actions as being part of a greater community unit beyond their immediate family and friends is vital if they are going to become effective and valuable citizens.

> 'A community is like a ship; everyone ought to be prepared to take the helm.'
> Henrik Ibsen

Community exercise for 'me'

Building your network of support – Take the advice from around the table from the last exercise and find a group, organization or community who can assist you or whom you can assist.

For example, if you want to learn Spanish, where can you go to find a night-class – a local school or college? Do you know someone who has learnt Spanish? Ask them. When we make our dreams public, it is surprising how many connections will reveal themselves to support us. One of the benefits of widening the network of our community is that someone always knows someone, who knows someone. The starting point for igniting this network of possible help and support is you. Take action. Take action everyday towards your goal. You do not have to know the exact route between you and your dream but you do need to take the first step. Or, in the words of Martin Luther King: 'Take the first step in faith. You don't have to see the whole staircase, just take the first step.'

Community exercise for 'we'

Getting to know you – If you want to know who is part of your community you had better go out and meet them. What message do we give our children about being part of a community if we only associate with our own 'tribe'? If we, the adults, only associate with our family or group this will raise the question in the mind of our children what is wrong with the rest of the world? If they do not have the actual experiences of being with others of different ages, cultures, colours or opinions then they run the risk of allowing their perceptions to misinform reality.

Around the table pose the question 'Where shall we go and who shall we see?' Encourage the family to suggest places or things that they have not been to or seen that they would like to find out about. Then do what you can to arrange a visit or experience for them to have their perception challenged, changed or confirmed.

I remember, some years ago, when my eldest daughter Lily was 8 she returned home from her C of E school talking very enthusiastically about a lesson she had had on the

five pillars of Islam. They had looked at pictures of Mosques and exotic places and people. She asked if she could be a Muslim as they dress nicely. I had no objection in principle but thought she might like to find out a bit more. So, I invited a friend and work colleague of mine up from London to join us in rural Northants. I have three daughters and Azam has two girls of similar ages to my oldest two.

We prepared a lovely lunch for Azam and his family and the girls were very excited about meeting 'real' Muslims and had made a great effort with helping prepare the food.

When they arrived around 1pm the girls proudly announced that they had made food for them all. Azam smiled and taking me to one side asked if we could postpone the eating till after sunrise as it was Ramadan and they were fasting.

Well, I could not have asked for a better means of generating questions and for the rest of the day the children played and asked questions of each other's world. They did this in the clear, direct and uninhibited way that children do. The weekend was a great success.

The point of that short personal account is that within a few hours my children had their perception of an entire culture removed from being something vague and mysterious to being real. The reality of Islam for my children are the memories of spending a weekend with two engaging girls who looked different, fasted, prayed to God by another name but were as cheeky and as much fun as they were.

Take the family to places: museums, lakes, cities, the countryside, the seaside, churches, synagogues, mosques, swimming, fetes, festivals and farmers' markets, etc. Find a part of the community that they do not have much understanding of and go and shift their perception into reality. The danger is, if we are trapped by our own tribal attitude and do not want that expanded or challenged then we run the risk of passing the baton of prejudice, fear and ignorance onto our children.

What is good about the tribe could become a reason for rejection later on in the lives of our children if they feel that they have been denied exposure to other thoughts, sights and world views. If one is seeking to raise a family where they feel comfortable to think and challenge then to expose the whole family to new experiences is a must.

The negative thing about the 'community'-centred level is that it tends to reject hierarchies. It seeks equality and consensus which, while honourable and good, can mean that, at its most closed, community-orientated families do not evolve to the next level of complexity because their focus is on keeping everyone happy and not wanting disharmony. At the next level disharmony is not only accepted but seen as an essential element for evolution at every level.

Complexity/Interconnected

> 'Abandon the urge to simplify everything, to look for formulas and easy answers, and begin to think multidimensionally, to glory in the mystery and paradoxes of life, not to be dismayed by the multitude of causes and consequences that are inherent in each experience – to appreciate the fact that life is complex.'
> M. Scott Peck

And so to late teens/early twenties, when the shifting returns to self and the larger questions of life. Neurologically, the adult brain fully develops (but does not stop its capacity to change) around the mid-twenties. While the community-centred existence brings us many things: belonging, safety, purpose, support, etc; it also runs the risk, if we become closed, that our thinking can become stagnant because we do not want to upset the group. When we confuse 'equality' with 'fairness' we may end up doing nothing because it may upset the sensitivities of others. On the face of it, a community-centred group is there to build something for the greater good. Their whole existence is about sharing love and happiness with the world. But what if they have not got the whole picture? What if (heaven help us) they are wrong? What if their belief system and driver for the existence of that group was brought into question? Well, they (we) have a choice: take on the new learning and apply it. This does not mean rejecting the level (or levels) that have gone before, but rather 'embrace and evolve'.

Let us apply a little more complexity to this situation and see where it takes us. At this next level of human existence we are seeking to see the interconnectivity of things and how the individual fits into it all. This is a 'me'-centred state. We do not mind questioning because we have a genuine desire to discover our role in the world. We challenge what went before and the belief systems of parents, elders and the community that we are a part of.

This is dangerous stuff if the community and family of which you are part are closed and therefore see you as a threat. When challenge happens to our thinking or in our world we will find ourselves moving to a level where we feel safe. In certain closed scenarios, if you question the validity of the rules you may find yourself, your safety and your success challenged.

Mahatma Gandhi is a good example. He could see that trying to fit into the system imposed by the British during the occupation would be complicated and impractical. When he challenged the injustices and limitations imposed on India's people, the dominant tribe (the British government) attacked him and his followers with tragic consequences.

While our personal family difficulties are not at the same global level as Gandhi's, they are still painful. If we are rejected by our close society, who or what will sustain us? If we see things from a long-term perspective and on a more interconnected level, we may take that step away from the community, knowing that our reason for challenge may lead us to return to the group with a greater capacity to serve it.

At this level we also, due to our capacity to see the world in a more complex and interconnected way, are more inclined to use the positive aspects of all the levels to our advantage. Someone centred at this level of complexity can use a bird's-eye view to observe the situation in which they find themselves and choose the course of action that would best serve their goals. If they are working with an individual or group that is very rooted in the tribal mode then they would present their ideas in tribal language. Should they have a challenge with their adolescent son or daughter, they would seek to assess where they are coming from first and then engage with them at that level. Not, as so often happens, try to insist that their child sees their point-of-view, or just does as they are told.

> 'We cannot expect that all nations will adopt like systems, for conformity is the jailer of freedom and the enemy of growth.' John Fitzgerald Kennedy

When we find ourselves resorting to 'do this because I say so' statements (and I accept that some times we have to), we are in the egocentric level ourselves, maybe with a bit of order-based authority. When we adapt our thinking and behaviour to fit and manage the complexity of the circumstances in which we find ourselves, whatever they are, then – and only then – are we working at a 'mature' level.

If we are 'open' at this level then we move with more fluidity within a world that is constantly shifting – we have a hand upon the helm and can influence the direction in which we go. We also find that once we have centred ourselves in this state, we not only enjoy the journey with greater insight, but we have shifted our world view sufficiently that we can reflect upon our own childhood with greater understanding and compassion.

> 'We shall not cease from exploration, but the end of our exploring, will be to arrive at the place we started and to know it for the first time.' T. S. Eliot

Interconnected exercise for 'me'

Deepen your network and open up your path – Having started the ball rolling by investigating people and places in your community that can help you to achieve your goals, build on this. You will find more and more links to getting what you want. Let people know what you want and need and expect the best outcome.

Have a goal in mind and take action every day to move towards it by drawing from the links that are out there but you may not have accessed yet. Speak to other parents when you drop the kids off. Use the internet to see if there is anything going on in your area to support you. You would be surprised. I have just typed 'Salsa Dancing in Northampton' into Google and have instantly accessed about 370,000 possible sources. The internet is a great vehicle for finding hooks into our community both local and global. But you are the person who has to take action.

If you have not taken action yet and gone out to your community then you are going to be limiting the possible connections of support. Interconnectivity in the form of networks of support is just one way of revealing the reality of this level of existence. I am not sure how it works but it does. The starting point, as Patanjali points out, is having a dream that you are passionate about.

> 'When you are inspired by some great purpose, some extraordinary project, all your thoughts break their bonds: Your mind transcends limitations, your consciousness expands in every direction, and you find yourself in a new, great, and wonderful world. Dormant forces, faculties and talents become alive, and you discover yourself to be a greater person by far than you ever dreamed yourself to be.' Patanjali

Interconnected exercise for 'we'

Looking backwards from a point of victory – This final exercise is based on one that went down well as part of a series I did for the BBC called *The Confidence Lab*.[12] We had a very positive response to the programme and in particular to this exercise. I have adapted it as a family game. Do this exercise once the meal is over. Leave the TV off and get back to a bit of good old Victorian parlour games with a more modern and problem-solving focus.

We called this exercise the 'Ten Chairs' game for goal setting and success but let's just go for five and focus on short- and medium-term goals.

Put five chairs in a line next to each other and get one family member to sit in the chair at one end. This represents where they are now on a timeline. Ask them to 'travel through time' and connect with the future. It can be anytime in the future but, for the purpose of this exercise, aim for a three-month goal. When they are in the chair they need to describe where they are. This is going to be a place where they have achieved, or have reached a goal towards their greater objective. For example they might want to be get a good grade for the maths exam they are taking in nine months so where are they on this path at three months?

They need to make it as clear a picture as possible. Using the five senses is a good tick list. What can they see (a test sheet with A written on it), smell (the classroom where they have been given the paper), taste (the water they have been drinking more of to help their concentration), touch (the feel of the paper) or hear (congratulations of the teacher and friends at achieving such a noticeable improvement)? Also how do they feel? Excited? Relieved? Proud?

When they have described the positive place bring them closer to now by moving down a chair in time. The time could be weeks or days; be flexible. Focus on key targets. For example, if they are going for great grades in maths by Week 12 (Chair 5) then the other chairs may look like this:

Chair 4 – Week 10 – They have stuck to their revision timetable and have just done a mock test and it was easy. To achieve that they had to create a revision timetable.

Chair 3 – Week 3 – They now have a clear timetable of what they are going to revise and when and feel able to balance study with the rest of their lives without getting stressed. In order to do this they asked for help.

Chair 2 – Tomorrow – They are going to sit down with a friend, teacher or family member and start creating a timetable. Back to Chair 1.

Chair 1 – Here and now.

If they do not do what they need to do tomorrow then they are unlikely to achieve their three, ten and twelve-week goals.

This is a very powerful tool to highlight that when we have clear goals and an action plan that is realistic and focused we will get to our destination. This about planning, problem solving and having a bit of humility to ask for help when needed. When we are able to draw, effectively, on the connections of friends and family and combine this with structure, discipline, imagination and vision then we will achieve our goals.

Indeed if it was not for the support of my wife Angie, who has been an amazing friend and support during the writing of this book it would never have happened. During my periods of doubt and frustration she has provided me with the encouragement and clarity that I needed.

Families do not have to be just the blood relatives in your life. A family can be made of family friends who act as if they were family. These people are rare treasures and I am delighted to say that we have a few of them who make up our wider 'family'. One of them, Emma Kilbey, has been an amazing friend who has looked over my contribution to this book with a keen, intelligent, critical and creative eye. Her input has generated some serious rethinking and rewriting which, although a challenge, has been rewarding for me (and I hope for you). Thanks Em.

To me, this is further testimony of the need to have a family around you who will listen, challenge and support you when you need to make a shift through those periods of frustration. In fact the process of evolution demands a degree of frustration and friction and families certainly provide lots of that. Without this dynamic friction we would never evolve. We need, at each level, to feel uncomfortable and ill at ease otherwise we have no motivation for change. This leads me onto the last level that I will dwell on to any degree – interdependent.

Interdependent

'General Systems Theory ... says that each variable in any system interacts with the other variables so thoroughly that cause and effect cannot be separated. A simple variable can be both cause and effect. Reality will not be still. And it cannot be taken apart! You cannot understand a cell, a rat, a brain structure, a family, a culture if you isolate it from its context. Relationship is everything.'
Marilyn Ferguson, The Aquarian Conspiracy

It would be fair to say that this level of human existence is usually attained once we have been 'around the block' a few times. For some people that may be in their late 20s. For others it will be in their late 30s/early 40s. For many it will be much later, for some earlier – and some never. I would like to point out that while I now have a grasp of this level from the point of view of Rumer Godden's four rooms (physical, mental, emotional and spiritual), up until recently, my understanding of this level of interdependence was very much at an intellectual level. By that I mean my logical reasoning (based on the sequential and exponential evolutionary process in Graves' theory) deduced that a 'we'-centred 'interdependent' existence would be the next stage. It would also have to be a 'we'-centred level that is more intellectually, practically, emotionally and spiritually evolved then the earlier 'we' levels.

'We eventually learn that spirituality is not about leaving life's problems behind, but about continually confronting them with honesty and courage. It is about ending our feeling of separation from others by healing our relationships with parents, co-workers and friends. It is about bringing heightened awareness and compassion to our family life, careers, and community service.' J. Krishnamurti

For the purpose of this book I only need to touch on this level, but would rather seek to direct our efforts, as parents, to the earlier levels. If we have older children (25+) then maybe this interdependent state is where we should centre our relationship. This is assuming that both parents and children have worked their way successfully through the other levels.

A word of warning here! Some people may aspire so strongly to reach this level of 'enlightenment' that they think they've got there without fully journeying through the rest of the spiral. They may have attained a higher level 'intellectually' or 'spiritually' (whatever that means) but have distanced themselves 'emotionally' from the rest of the world and their family and have great difficulty manifesting this enlightened state in a 'practical' form. This brings us back to Godden again.

Imagine these four core intelligences as elevators moving up the levels of human existence. To be truly embedded and secure at each level we should be able to change lifts at each level and still be capable of travelling to whichever floor we need. Some of us prefer one or two lifts. We may be drawn to the intellectual or spiritual lift, but have reservations about one of the others. We may excel in the practical application of ideas, but not be comfortable with emotional openness and honesty. We may have to go down a few floors to engage or repair one of the four rooms. The older we get, the harder we may find this. If we have reached an age where we haven't developed one of the four core intelligences we will run the risk of believing that this is just 'who I am'. We may become entrenched in a world view that not only limits our own happiness and success, but also gives the signal to our children that it is OK to stop growing up. When we 'cease our exploration' then we are indicating to our children that there's a finite, 'grown-up' point where they can stop, too.

The harsh reality is that life demands that we adapt and evolve. We do not 'grow up'. We will never get to a point when everything in the garden is rosy. We might have days or even weeks when everything works in our favour and we can enjoy the fruits of our labours, but there will inevitably come a point when we have to get up and start work again. This is just life.

Graves provides us not only with a hierarchy of evolution, he also has provided the steps to manage each transition:

1. Potential in the system.

2. Solutions to problems of present level.

3. Dissonance about present state.

4. Insight into alternatives.

5. Barriers identified and dealt with.

6. Consolidation and support in the new state.

All the stages I have summarized in this section from survival to interdependent have required us to engage in those six steps. When we see these stages as necessary for our advancement then the evolution of ourselves and that of our family will be more likely to be in the direction of happiness and success than unhappiness and failure.

When we see the surface behaviours of our siblings, partners, parents and children in the light of Spiral Dynamics we will, as a consequence of this understanding, be more tolerant, supportive and appreciative. This is what any family that seeks to be genuinely happy desires.

The key to approaching the development of all these levels is to be open in our thoughts, feelings, actions and intuition. When we can look dispassionately through the Graves model of human existence we can then see the influences on our own parents and maybe realize that they did the best with what they had and what they knew.

I am not going to include exercises for this level. If you are centred here then you may have discovered appropriate ones for yourself. What I will do is remind you of the following quote from Graves. Hopefully, having read not only my chapter but those written by Tim, Trish and Steve, the words will have more resonance and meaning for you than when you first started reading.

> 'As he [or she] sets off on each quest, he believes he will find the answer to his existence, and as he settles into each nodal state he is certain he has found it. Yet, always to his surprise and ever to his dismay he finds, at every stage, that the solution to existence is not the solution he thinks he has found. Every state he reaches leaves him discontented and perplexed. It is simply that as he solves one set of human problems, he finds a new set in their place. The quest he finds is never-ending.' [13]

By reading this book you have hopefully gained some practical tools to support the development of your children and yourself. Oliver Wendell Holmes said about new ideas that: 'A mind once stretched by a new idea, cannot return to its original dimensions.'

Obviously a mind can only be stretched if it is open. If you have sought to read this book to confirm your own world view I hope that at some point we have challenged it. If you have dismissed anything that you found uncomfortable without reflection, questioning and application do not close the book here but go back to the beginning and re-read. I guarantee that on a second reading, even more meaning and messages will reveal themselves to you.

Footnotes and further reading

1. Graves, Clare W. (2002) *Levels of Human Existence. A Transcription*, edited by William R. Lee, Christopher Cowan and Natasha Todorovic. California: ECLET Publishing.

2. Chris and Natasha have produced, in my opinion, the definitive book on Gravesian theory, *Clare W. Graves: The Never Ending Quest,* which is a compilation of his unfinished manuscripts plus other writings.

3. © 1999 Copyright NVC Consulting used with permission. www.spiraldynamics.org. For information about UK programmes in Spiral Dynamics go to www.thebeyondpartnership.com.

4. Toffler, Alvin (1984), *Future Shock*. London: Bantam.

5. www.21stcenturyskills.org.

6. Handy, Charles (1998), *The Hungry Spirit.* London: Arrow Books.

7. I am not going to swamp you with masses of child brain stuff but, if you are interested, have a look at *The Big Book of Independent Thinking* (Crown House Publishing, 2006). There is an excellent chapter on the brain by Dr Andrew Curran (there is also a rather good chapter on the myth of intelligence by one R. Leighton).

8. www.developingchild.net/pubs/persp/deprivation/deprivation_and_disruption_3.html.

9. www.teachingexpertise.com/articles/the-importance-of-physical-touch-1628.

10. Toffler, Alvin (1989), *The Third Wave*. London: Bantam.

11. If you are interested in finding out how you or your child learn I would recommend you complete the appropriate level Learning Style Assessment (LSA) by going to www.clc.co.nz.

12. If you want a link go to www.bbc.co.uk/health/confidence/learn. The book accompanying the series is also available: *Confidence in Just Seven Days* (London: Vermilion, 2001).

13. Graves, Clare W. (2002) *Levels of Human Existence. A Transcription*, edited by William R. Lee, Christopher Cowan and Natasha Todorovic. California: ECLET Publishing.

Index